"Universal Marriage and Relationship Tips"

Volume 1

by Brother Marcus and Sister Cecelia

We dedicate this book to our beloved Minister, who has taught us everything that we know, our parents, our relatives and our much beloved, children. We also dedicate this book to couples who are doing well in their marriages and relationships but they are looking for ways to improve what they already have. Wives need better skills to bring out of their husbands the best in them and certainly, husbands need better skills to bring out the best in our women... We should make it our goal to leave our women smiling and happy because we happened to come their way...

> **❝I like it when a guy makes me feel like a woman and a litte girl ❞ at the same time.**
>
> *Tara Reid*

Foreword

There is no success in building a nation without the building of family. There is no success in the building of family without the respect and honor for the institution of marriage. Do we really know enough about how to make a marriage work in this day and time? We want to be with the love of our lives forever, and they with you, but we are so busy! Why and how do we always make our marriages a top priority? Why did God originate marriage in the first place and do we really have enough respect for what the Creator originated? We begin the real journey of life through the institution of marriage when we declare our desire to become as **one**.

Since God is **One,** the universe is **one**, the only way that marriage can be successful is for the man and woman to strive to become as **one**. For the man to see the woman as an object of pleasure or to further him in procreation is only partially seeing the purpose of God's creation of the female. The strengthening of the union of the male and the female in the institution of marriage is the best preparation for the production of family.

Presented here are some easy and fun ways to keep improving an already awesome partnership. Even if you're not married yet, you can start practicing these tips to enjoy your relationship even more throughout the wedding-planning process. Grooms and husbands, should read and hold onto this book as well — these same rules apply to you, too! This book may prove invaluable to you if no one has ever shared this kind of wisdom with you.

Our teacher has shared with us that, **"Our commitment to strong marriage secures our nation".** May the universal marriage tips contained in Volume 1 of this series, strengthen your marriage relationships forever.

Brother Marcus and Sister Cecelia

Marriage Tip #1

People often ask Sister Cecelia and I, **"How do we learn to make our marriage successful?"** And here is the simple answer that we always give… Put God first in your marriage! Always! He will help both of you to navigate all the details of your union.

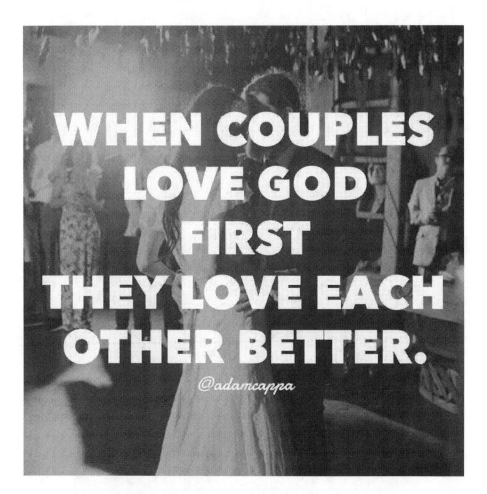

WHEN COUPLES LOVE GOD FIRST THEY LOVE EACH OTHER BETTER.
@adamcappa

Marriage Tip #2

Research consistently shows that touching more creates a stronger bond by releasing oxytocin. This hormone is sometimes known as the "cuddle hormone" or the "love hormone," because it is released when a couple snuggles up or bonds socially. Once you have entered into marriage you should hold hands, rub shoulders, hug, kiss, give high-fives or even fist-bumps as often as possible. Research suggests that when a marriage is in trouble, kissing is the first thing to go. Use your frequency of kissing as an index of the health of your marriage. When you give a quick hug or kiss, try to lengthen it to at least 5 or 10 seconds for more effective results! We should hug our children, male and female as much as possible; especially when they are older and they tend to start to pull away from us as parents.

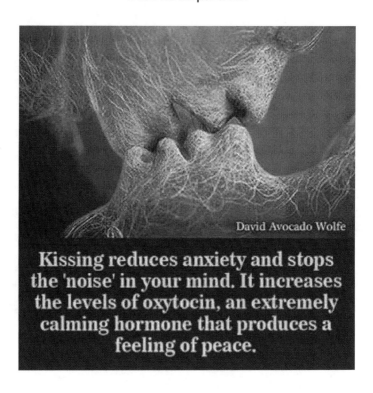

David Avocado Wolfe

Kissing reduces anxiety and stops the 'noise' in your mind. It increases the levels of oxytocin, an extremely calming hormone that produces a feeling of peace.

Marriage Tip #3

Learn how to agree to disagree in your marriage. If you operate the way most people do, when your spouse takes exception to your viewpoint—or introduces one sharply contrasting with yours—you may find it almost impossible NOT to experience them as invalidating you, personally attacking you, or striving to defeat you. And if this is how you perceive them in the moment—not as your lifetime companion but as your willful adversary—then you're compelled to strike back, defend yourself, or even exit the situation entirely, whether mentally, emotionally, or physically.

After all, in that instant of disagreement their words have managed to morph them into your enemy. How could this not be the case if, somewhere deep in your gut, you experience their contrary point of view as somehow puncturing your own?

(And incidentally, there's an awfully good chance they'll be reacting to you similarly—i.e., experiencing YOUR position as aiming poison arrows at theirs.)

No two people agree on everything, and that's okay, but it's important to be okay with each other's differences.

These four rules should be helpful.

Rule One: Discussions should take place only when both partners feel ready. If one spouse isn't prepared to talk, then that spouse must suggest another time in the near future.

Rule Two: One spouse has the floor at a time. It is important to begin the discussion on a positive note. 'Spouse A' speaks for no more than two or three sentences.

Rule Three: 'Spouse B' is the designated listener. It is the listener's task to make sure the speaker feels understood. 'Spouse B' should repeat what 'Spouse A' has heard to confirm it is what 'Spouse A' intended. 'Spouse B' is not to comment or react, just paraphrase 'Spouse A' comments back to him or her. 'Spouse A' then lets 'Spouse B' know whether what they said is accurate. If so, 'Spouse A' can make additional points. If not, 'Spouse A' repeats the point to help 'Spouse B' really hear what is being said. The speaker-listener interaction continues until 'Spouse A' has their point made. Then the speaker should ask the listener for feedback.

Rule Four: 'Spouse B' now has the floor, and 'Spouse A' becomes the designated listener. Partners can switch roles as often as is necessary to clarify points and feelings.

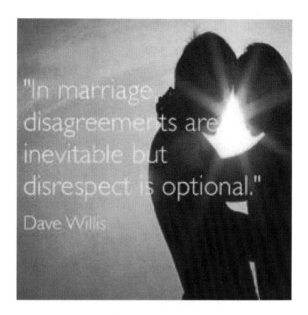

"In marriage disagreements are inevitable but disrespect is optional."

Dave Willis

When you have a disagreement with a loved one, I challenge you to say " I love you more than this argument"

~Katherine Miracle

Marriage Tip #4

Sometimes it's not about the amount of money you spend on a gift; it's about the thought that goes into something. Take the time to write a thoughtful note every so often saying what you love and appreciate about him/her. Drop it in his/her briefcase or purse so he/she will find it unexpectedly and it will brighten up his/her day. Receiving Gifts could be one of the primary love languages of your partner. Don't mistake this love language for materialism; the receiver of gifts thrives on the love, thoughtfulness, and effort behind the gift. If you speak this language, the perfect gift or gesture shows that you are known, you are cared for, and you are prized above whatever was sacrificed to bring the gift to you. A missed birthday, anniversary, or a hasty, thoughtless gift would be disastrous – so would the absence of everyday gestures. Gifts are visual representations of love and are treasured greatly. The next time you are out doing grocery shopping or running an errand, buy your better half something that reminds you of them. It doesn't have to be extravagant or expensive; the key is to let them know that you are thinking of them. Don't have extra cash? Pick a flower from your walk home or simply write him a letter by hand.

It's important to note: When you give a present, do you expect something in return? Are you giving these roses because you want forgiveness? Are you giving this box of chocolates because you want sex? Are you giving this I-Pad because you want a gift of equal value in return? If so, you've left the realm of gift giving and entered the realm of economic exchange. You're saying **"I will give you this if you give me that"**. You may not be saying it in those words but you may as well be. This kind of behaviour doesn't qualify as gift giving. Mutually beneficial exchanges are a strong part of every relationship and we have to be honest about what we want and when we want it from our spouses.

A real present doesn't carry any obligations with it. A present doesn't put the receiver in debt to you. It doesn't make the receiver feel like they owe you anything and it shouldn't be given with the thought of **"I'm giving this because I expect something in return."** Even in our marriages we have to learn to do no favour seeking gain...

Marriage Tip #5

For men, it's important to understand that wives truly want to be listened to. Husbands don't need to solve or fix everything; listening itself is an exceptional gift. If you truly want to increase your impact in your marriage and accomplish even better results, become a master at listening. For women, it's important to understand that men need time for themselves and a husband is not another girlfriend. By giving him space to pull away and not taking it personally, you allow him to reconnect with his desire for you and his commitment to the relationship. Some men have a great deal of difficulty validating and emotionally supporting the women in their lives, including their wives. Here are some of the reasons.

1. **Some men see marriage as a Power Struggle.** Some men view their intimate relationship as a win-lose game.
2. **Sarcasm.** Many men describe their interactions in terms of "sarcastic" comments -- put-downs, contempt, criticism and condescension.
3. **Macho Thinking**. A number of men comment that to validate or to use emotional language to support the woman is unmanly.
4. **Emotionally Troubling**. Some men find it so upsetting, so emotionally arousing to listen to their partners that they feel they have to ventilate their anger or withdraw.
5. **Not Wanting to Reinforce Whining.** This is another reason that men give for not supporting or encouraging expression.
6. **Demand for Rationality.** Some men believe that their partner should always be rational and that irrationality cannot be tolerated.

7.   **Problems Have to Be Solved.** These men think that the main reason for communication is to share facts that then can be used for problem-solving. All seven of these statements have to be worked on by husbands who truly want to connect with their wives in the way Almighty God has naturally constructed women.

Marriage Tip #6

The biggest waste of effort in a marriage is trying to change your spouse, since the problems you have with your spouse are generally problems you have in yourself.
There are primarily two reasons why people might want to change your spouse.

(1) You want to see your spouse replicate your actions. If you squeeze the toothpaste from the bottom of the tube, or put the toilet seat cover down, you probably want your spouse to do so, too. *It's easy to approach differences with the attitude that your way is the right way. This attitude has ruined many a great marriage.*

(2) You want your spouse to meet your needs. *The more needy you are, the more likely you have a detailed agenda of what you want those changes to look like.*

When you try to change your spouse you come across as a nag and wind up sending the message that 'who you are is not enough.' Nobody likes getting that message, and it leads to distance and polarization. Let your spouse be who he or she is and focus on changing yourself. Our marriage changed for the better when Brother Marcus turned all the energy he was exerting into fixing Sister Cecelia onto himself and began working to fix him.

Marriage Tip #7

See problems — boredom in the bedroom, lack of conversations, resentment — as symptoms and treat those symptoms just as you would treat a chronic illness that seemingly has no cure. Most marriages find a crack in them when the partners become complacent. Ask yourself what can I do today to make my spouse smile? Ask yourself, **"Am I doing my part in this marriage relationship?"** By God's grace, we have been given the keys to our spouse's peace and security but if we don't lock that car, somebody will steal it. Never say, **"I know that my spouse is happy!"** People change constantly and so do morals, up your game and make sure that you keep the ink fresh on that marriage certificate. It's important to know that all marriages are imperfect and most of them are imperfect in exactly the same ways. The list of marital problems you encounter in a healthy marriage isn't so long and most of them are pretty manageable. No matter what your challenges are in your marriage... throw at it every possible remedy you've got, no matter how alternative or weird it seems. Chances are one or more of them will actually work and your marriage will get stronger and stronger.

Marriage Tip #8

Using good communication skills helps keep an argument from escalating and emotions under control. Fear, hurt, and anger lead to shouting, name-calling, and tears - problem magnifiers that interfere with communication and add fuel to an already heated situation. The next time you argue with your partner, drop the shaming, blaming, needing to be right, and really listen without interrupting. Then communicate how you feel, using "I" statements. It's not your partner's job to read your mind, guess what you're thinking, or put words into your mouth. These are huge obstacles to open, honest communication and will guarantee resentment, anger, and frustration in the relationship. Remember what the wise men and women have taught us, **"Too much arguing drives the spirit of Almighty God out of the marriage or the relationship."**

How Emotions Harm *YOU.*

MOST OF THE THINGS YOU WORRY ABOUT NEVER HAPPEN!

* **Anger** : *Weakens The Liver*
* **Grief**: *Weakens The Lung*
* **Worry** : *Weakens The Stomach*
* **Stress** : *Weakens The Heart & Brain*
* **Fear** : *Weakens The Kidney*

Marriage Tip #9

In order to strengthen your marriage, learn to recognize that most arguments have shared responsibility, that both people have valid points and valid reasons for their feelings. **So when you shoot an arrow of truth at your spouse, make sure you dip its point in honey. We all have to remember, even in the heat of battle, truth is the authority in the marriage and not biology.** What qualifies as fighting fair in marriage essentially comes down to how each partner feels when they leave the ring. If both are hearty "boxers" who love a few rounds in the ring and then can come back to being peaceful, that's one thing. But if people leave the ring angry, bitter, and resentful, perhaps it's time to re-evaluate.

How to keep the peace in your marriage and smooth things over:
*Pray. Be humble and talk to God about your situation and be open to hear His voice and reasoning. You can also go and read His word.
*Remember that going to bed angry might be the best choice. It allows partners to clear their thoughts, get some sleep, and make a date to resume the fight (which might seem less important in the light of day).
*Take a break. Even a 30-minute break can help a couple push the reset button on a fight. Stop, step out of the room, and reconnect when everyone's a little calmer.
*Own up to your part of the fight. Two things derail intense fights: admitting what you did to get your partner ticked off and expressing empathy toward your partner. This can be difficult but is typically extremely successful. Letting down our defenses in the heat of battle seems counterintuitive, but it is actually very effective with couples.
*Find the humor, if you can, in whatever it is that you and your spouse are disagreeing about.
*Shut up and touch. Sometimes there's a point where discussing the matter doesn't help. So couples need to just hold each other when nothing else seems to be working. Reconnecting through

touch is very important. One thing we have both learned, "You can't argue naked"

*Ban the "but." Couples often derail a resolution when they acknowledge the other partner's position and then add a "but" in their next breath, reaffirming their own.

Marriage Tip #10

Fair is not a four letter word. You may have forgotten about fairness, but now's the time to bring it back into your relationship. Whether disgruntled or disheartened, the spouse feeling abused will experience ever-increasing alienation from their mate, if not downright antagonism toward them. And this is why it's so important for couples to be able to discuss openly—and with as much calmness and compassion as possible—how equitable or "just" each of them perceives the union. Are you both being fair when it comes to divvying up chores, communicating your needs, expressing dissatisfaction, dealing with finances, parenting, and supporting one another? If not, how can you improve and bring fairness back to the relationship?

Marriage Tip #11

Nothing is more important in a marriage than the relationship between husband and wife. When other things become more important, such as careers, children, and personal pursuits, trouble sets in. Make the relationship your top priority. When you do, the marriage flourishes. Here is how you can make your marriage a top priority:

Commitment. Words are just words if we can't show our love through our actions. The commitment to living out your vows on a daily basis will help you place your marriage as top priority. Once you say 'I do' you can't cross your arms and wait. Because marriage is work.... and a lifelong commitment.

Your children will be affected. Not only are you experiencing your marriage but so are your children. You are their role models. Be a positive role model for your children as a parent and also as a united front for your marriage.

United front. No matter what comes your way, you'll know that you can rely on your spouse to support and love you. When you don't place your marriage as top priority, you'll have to experience life's challenges by yourself. Your spouse should be the one that you can bounce around ideas with and help you make the right decisions. When the two of you are working as a team, not only will you be able to get through the difficulties of life, but your marriage will deepen as a result.

Decrease the possibility of infidelity. When you and your spouse have a strong, committed, and healthy relationship, you won't have to look outside of the marriage to fulfill your needs. You don't always have to like each other, but you have to be committed. When you place your marriage as top priority, you will constantly be thinking, *"What is best for my marriage?"*

Future. If you haven't placed your marriage as top priority then how you can possibly stand to be with each other when your children grow up? If you've invested so much emotional energy into your children instead of your spouse, what will happen when your children grow up? People who don't have a strong and healthy relationship with their spouse tend to invest a lot into their children.

Marriage Tip #12

Are you creating more pleasurable interactions in your marriage or are you making it painful or unpleasant for your spouse? If your spouse treats you with kindness, gentleness, patience and self-control, it's easy for you to respond kindly. It's important to be kind to your spouse. Not a single person in the entire world would marry if he thought his partner would not treat him with kindness and vice versa. Marriage is a voluntary institution; a married individual must continually choose to stay with his or her partner. This is the reality of relationships whether we agree with it or not. When kindness is abundant within the relationship, the choice to stay together is easy. Kindness ensures peace in the home. Kindness is the fertile soil in which affection grows. Kindness is the foundation upon which a strong and healthy family is built. If you are treated badly, with anger, impatience, etc., it's difficult to be nice in return. Focus on how you can be a blessing to your spouse and, in turn, you will be blessed and so will your marriage.

random acts of Kindness

Marriage Tip #13

Expressing feelings in a relationship is very important. Feelings are at the heart of every marriage. Never begin a sentence with the word 'you'. Instead start with the word "I" and then share your feelings instead of your thoughts. This is not as easy as it sounds because we all disguise a lot of thoughts as feelings, as in **"I feel like you are avoiding me."** Here is another example of what disguising thoughts as feelings: **"I feel... that you don't want to be with me".** The problem with this form of communication is that the speaker does not take into consideration that their feelings are an interpretation, a perception of something that the other person has said, done or didn't do. The conversation is no longer about his/her feeling but about their perception. You can't feel that he or she doesn't want to be with you because a feeling is something entirely internal to you. You can only interpret based on your partner's behavior that it is a sign they don't want to be with you.

This way of conversing immediately makes the other person take a defensive mode, trying to prove that he or she actually wants to be with you. In theory, you get the reassurance that you want, but in reality, it ends up going very bad. After such communication, the speaker never feels they were able to fully express themselves because the conversation is no longer about feeling. It is about interpretation of the behavior. Genuine feelings are sad, angry, happy, lonely, frustrated, etc ... and sharing your core feelings creates better communication, and more connection and compassion. Strive to be sure that the emotion that you are most expressing as a spouse is not "anger".

Marriage Tip #14

Change your focus to one of learning to appreciate your partner. Here are a few tips for creating a list of the things that you appreciate about your partner:

(1) List all of your partner's intangible qualities, like generosity, honesty, and kindness. Another might be to focus on specific things your partner does that you love – regularly preparing dinner, for example, or helping you remember important appointments that always seem to slip your mind. If you want, your list can be a mix of intangible and concrete things. At first, it may be difficult to create a list, especially if you've grown annoyed by much of what your long-term partner does. Eliminate that block by reflecting on your differences in a positive light. All too often, couples grow accustomed to snapping at each other for handling life's demands in ways that, to the partner, are **"wrong."** Sometimes they very well may be wrong, but other times they might simply be different. It is worth noting that there is far more right going on with your husband or your wife than what is wrong with them... And there is far more right going on in your marriage than what is wrong about your marriage... It's important to maintain perspective.
(2) Another step to appreciating your partner again is to learn to embrace their quirks without taking them to be negative.
(3) Tap into your memory to find positive experiences you shared, too. Are there some warm moments that stand out, or a funny situation, or a difficult one that you both got through together. Reflect on the qualities your partner contributed to the situation that made it so memorable. Chances are they are the same traits that you should still be appreciating.
(4) After you have created your list, don't keep it to yourself! Let your partner know how much you appreciate them, and why. For an old-fashioned touch, write a hand-written letter that can be read over and over again. You could also tell them over a nice meal, or in the evening when you know they had a rough day.

> A woman can't change a
> man because she loves him,
> a man changes himself
> because he loves her.

Marriage Tip #15

Let go of criticism and blame. Hands down, we feel most compelled to request **"a talk"** with our partner, deliver a **"constructive"** criticism, or give unsolicited **"feedback"**, at the peak of our own emotional storm. When our mood is low and our defenses are high is when it feels most appropriate—and necessary, even—to talk it out. Ironically, that's also when it is least helpful to do so.

We all tend to do this. Our minds might be racing, full of:
"I-can't-believe-he/she…," and
"Something-needs-to-be-done…" thoughts,
and jumping into action feels not only wise, but required. After all, if I don't say something now, what will happen next time? If we don't discuss this, it will just fester and grow, right? But, letting things go does not mean they fester and grow.

Not all, but most "problems" in a relationship are problems in thinking. They are problems only because—and only when—one partner is thinking about them.

When our mood shifts (as moods always do) and our thinking clears (as thinking always does), the problem often vanishes. Of course we are not talking about major issues. But when we are about to lecture our spouses for the umpteenth time about this or that, that's a mood-induced **"problem"** brought on only by my current thinking. And we know that it's only a problem in our current thinking because when our mood is high and we are feeling great, it's not such a problem. So be careful of your mood in your marriage and remember that there are a whole lot of things that we are not really radically affected by.

Focus on what there is to appreciate about your mate, then honestly and spontaneously express your specific appreciation to them. It's also good to do this for yourself.

And then my soul saw you and it kind of went "Oh there you are. I've been looking for you."

Marriage Tip #16

Never lose the fine art of courting. Setting aside a romantic evening on a regular basis can rekindle the magic of a long-term relationship. It doesn't have to be fancy, just special time for the two of you to remember how and why you first fell in love. Here's how you can approach "rekindling"

1. **Let down your guard and let each other in again.** If you are really disconnected and passion has waned for some time, defensiveness and anger may well have taken loving connections place. Surrender your toughness and soften up to each other.

2. **Create a "rekindle" attitude.** Make reaching out and pursuing each other your priority and being playful and flirtatious as you once were your focus. So many couples have seemingly forgotten how to flirt and inject energy into the relationship -- that once upon a time came so easily. Flirt with your spouse again.

3. **Identify "passion builders" together that keep positive, exciting energy alive with your lover.** Certainly a vibrant sex life helps, but so does positive communication, attention to each other's wants and needs on a daily basis and having fun together with your clothes on. As far as the sex goes, change it up with novelty -- perhaps sex with your socks and hat on, or going out on a date pretending you've never met -- where you go all out in righteously seducing one another. After the sex act is over, we both want to feel good about ourselves.

4. **Construct a calendar that honors the need to keep love and passion alive.** Don't let your children or anything interfere with keeping your marriage the number 1 priority and growing and deepening your love life.

5. **Think of your marriage as a "tepee" where you grow and protect love.** Don't let anything or anyone in your tee pee that could get in the way of your sacred connection to each other! Keep your love out of the "cloud."

Marriage Tip #17

Have regular times, even if it's just for 15 minutes, to check in with each other. **One researcher found that happy couples "talked to each other frequently — not just about their relationship, but about other things."** We should set aside time every day to talk about anything other than work, family, the household or the relationship. This small change infuses relationships with new life. No talk about your children, schedules, etc. allowed. It can be difficult to stay connected to our loved ones in today's hectic world. We struggle to keep friendships strong with coffee dates and quick emails, and we diligently pencil in phone calls to our grandparents even when we're swamped. But our romantic relationships rarely receive the same type of attention that our friends and families do, and the results can be devastating. Imagine looking across the kitchen table at the familiar contours of your spouse's face... and realizing that the man / woman you married now feels like a total stranger. **Often couples forget to prioritize their time together.** Other activities like work, school, church / mosque, volunteering and hobbies take precedence. Suddenly every available moment is over-scheduled and the only time the couple shares together are spent sleeping. If this sounds too familiar to you or your spouse what will you do about it?

Guard yourselves against overcommitment.

It causes damage to relationships.

Marriage Tip #18

Love your marriage by first taking care of yourself. Take care of in all arenas but particularly, take care of yourself physically and spiritually. That way, your stress will be down and your tolerance will be up. You'll be less likely to get on each other's nerves -- and to squabble. You're more likely to have a happy marriage. Many spouses say the reason their marriage fell apart is that they became depressed and disinterested in their partner. **The road to divorce is paved with eye rolls, the silent treatment, and poor communication in general.**

Below, divorce attorneys and marriage therapists have shared some of the most damaging things you can say in a marriage.

1. **"You're being ridiculous."** Dismissing your spouse's feelings as "ridiculous" runs counter to striving your very hardest to understand your partner's perspective.
2. **"I don't care anymore."**
A clear marker on the pathway to divorce is when one or both spouses become disinterested in the actions of the other because it's such a blunt way to convey your disinterest.
3. **"You never help out around the house."**
You're in the danger zone whenever you let the words **"always"** or **"never"** slip into a conversation with your spouse, whatever the issue may be.
4. **"If you hadn't forgotten to pick up the dry cleaning, I wouldn't have to yell at you."** Dry cleaning is a placeholder here: The issue you're arguing about could be anything. Whatever your issue is, blaming your partner for your reaction is bound to provoke them and cause resentment.
5. **Nothing at all.** Saying nothing at all -- or stonewalling your partner -- can cause more damage to your marriage than any statement on this list. Stonewalling occurs when one partner withdraws from the interaction or argument, closing themselves off to what the other spouse has to say.

6. ¨I want a divorce”. Did you think we'd make it through this list without mentioning the D word? It seems obvious, but threatening divorce when you don't really want one chips away at the foundation of your marriage.

7. "I don't need to tell you where I went." Your spouse shouldn't need to keep tabs on your whereabouts at all hours of the day, but there also shouldn't be a need for secrecy.

8. "Why can't you be more like him / her?" Stop making comparisons to other people's husbands or wives. Belittling your spouse by comparing him or her to another man or woman is a low blow.

9. "I wish I never met you." Few phrases are more devastating -- or damaging -- than this one. It's especially hurtful because it implies that your partner is to blame for every undesirable thing that's happened in your life since you first met.

The Four Horsemen (criticism, contempt, defensiveness, and stonewalling) predict early divorcing

5.6 YEARS AFTER THE WEDDING
(Gottman, J.M. 1994)

Emotional withdrawal, the absence of positive affect during conflict discussions (shared humor, affection, empathy) predict later divorcing

16.2 YEARS AFTER THE WEDDING
(Gottman, J.M. 1994)

The average couple waits

6 YEARS
before seeking help for marital problems.
(Gottman, J.M. 1994)

1/2
of all marriages that end do so in the first seven years.
(Gottman, J.M. 1994)

Stonewalling occurs when the listener enters Diffuse Physiological Arousal (DPA) and their heart rate exceeds 100 BPM.
(Gottman, J.M. 1994)

Dr. Gottman is able to predict with over

90% ACCURACY
which couples will divorce and which will stay together.
(Gottman, J.M. and Levenson, R. 2002)

69%
of conflict in relationships is about unresolvable, perpetual problems. 16% of these perpetual issues involve gridlocked couple conflict.
(Gottman, J.M. 1994)

85%
of stonewallers in heterosexual relationships are men.
(Gottman, J.M. 1994)

5:1   0.8:1

Dr. Gottman reports that stable marriages have a 5:1 ratio of positivity to negativity during conflict, whereas in unstable marriages the ratio is 0.8:1.
(Gottman, J.M. and Levenson, R. 1999)

80%
of the time, women bring up issues in heterosexual relationships.
(Gottman, J.M. 1994)

Dr. Gottman has completed 12 longitudinal studies with over 3,000 couples. The longest couples were followed for

20 YEARS
(Gottman, J.M. 1994)

67%
of new parents experience a precipitous drop in couple satisfaction in the first three years of the baby's life.
(Shapiro, A.F. and Gottman, J.M. 2005)

Sources:

Gottman, J.M., and Levenson, R.W. "What predicts change in marital interaction over time? A study of alternative models." Family Processes Journal. 38.2 (1999):143-58. Print.

Gottman, J.M., and Levenson, R.W. " A Two-Factor Model for Predicting When a Couple Will Divorce: Exploratory Analyses Using 14-Year Longitudinal Data." Family Processes Journal, 41.1 (2002): 83-96. Print.

Gottman, J.M., What Predicts Divorce? The Relationship Between Marital Processes and Marital Outcomes. Hillsdale, NJ: Lawrence Erlbaum Associates, 1994. Print.

Shapiro, A.F., and Gottman, "J.M. Effects on Marriage of a Psycho-Communicative-Educational Intervention with Couples Undergoing the Transition to Parenthood, Evaluation at 1-year Post Intervention." Journal of Family Communication 5.1 (2005):1-24. Print.

Marriage Tip #19

Recognize that your husband or wife is mirroring back to you who you are. Ever walk past a mirror and are shocked or mortified by what you see? Your hair standing up in a weird way, your slip showing, your fly open, egg stuck in your teeth? Mirrors can be real lifesavers. Had it not been for that mirror, you may have gone the entire day looking ridiculous. Marriage is a mirror. **By living so closely with another human being, you start to get a picture of what you really look like.** You start to see where you need to adjust and change. This is why marriage is so effective at making people's lives more rich and productive - if they adjust to the needed changes. It has been said that women marry a man expecting he will change, but he doesn't and that men marries a woman expecting that she won't change, but she does. **Unfortunately, many expect marriage to be something that makes them look better, not something that reveals where they don't look so good.** Additionally, rather than see where we need to change, we opt to project our own negative images on our spouses and point out where they need to change: She is so irritating....he is such a lazy slob....I don't want to act this way, but she brings out the worst in me. Take whatever you're upset with him/her about and use it to help yourself look squarely at what you need to do in order to grow and evolve—any maybe our relationship will thrive!

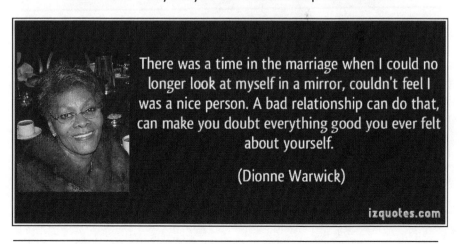

There was a time in the marriage when I could no longer look at myself in a mirror, couldn't feel I was a nice person. A bad relationship can do that, can make you doubt everything good you ever felt about yourself.

(Dionne Warwick)

izquotes.com

Marriage Tip #20

Take time to have some fun together every day! With today's hectic schedules, it's easy to find your marriage at the bottom of the priority list. Take a walk and hold hands (nature calms), cook a meal together, exercise together (tennis or dancing maybe?) or just collect a "Daily Joke" to share. **Successful couples enjoy each other.** It's just that simple. They like to be together, talk together, do things together. Because of this, there are less down days for the successful couple than up. They like spending a lot of time... together. It doesn't have to be expensive, but if you make the commitment and effort to laugh together as often as possible, it can sweeten your connection and cement your relationship for life.

The most successful marriages are those where both husband and wife seek to build the self-esteem of the other.

– Dr. James Dobson –

DrJamesDobson.org
#YourLegacyMatters

Marriage Tip #21

Before you get mad or assign blame, take a breath and ask your partner for his or her perspective. One of the most powerful and far reaching strategies for showing love for our spouse is to acknowledge, validate, and respect their point of view — even if it differs significantly from our own. We often do not take a look at challenging situations from our partner's point of view. Almost by definition, in a wide variety of areas, spouses will experience differences of opinion, and place different priorities on things. Spouses will likely exhibit different styles of parenting, experience different levels of sexual interest, have different preferences for managing and spending money, and prefer to spend time in different ways. We miss so much when we don't hear from our spouses, like opportunities to move forward and create solutions. Many times it is because we only care about our own perspective.

> 10% of conflict is due to difference in opinion and 90% is due to delivery & tone of voice.

Marriage Tip #22

Make a list of three of the happiest moments in your marriage. Spend a few minutes each day briefly reliving those moments in your mind. The results will amaze you. Relive the moments with your spouse and just laugh and laugh! Research reveals that couples who serve as cheerleaders for one another are not only more optimistic about life and love, but are far more likely to live happily ever after.

Out of all of the *moments* in my life... THE ONES *I've spent with you* are my most *favorite*

HappyWivesClub.com

Marriage Tip #23

You can change your relationship for the better by increasing the use of the following statements: **"I love you"**, **"I'm here for you"**, **"I understand"**, **"I'm sorry "**, **"Thank you"**, **"I really appreciate all that you do"**, **"It's so nice to see you"**, **"That was quite an accomplishment!"**

Are You
Speaking Words of Life
into
Your Marriage
or
Are You Tearing It Down?

Marriage Tip #24

Appreciate your partner at least five times each day. Appreciate them from your heart about who they are at their essence. Leave gratitude in love notes, hide them so they will find them, or look deeply into their eyes and tell them. Be creative!

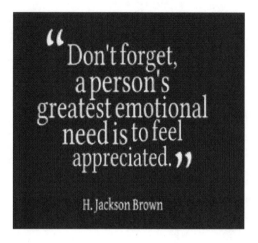

" Don't forget, a person's greatest emotional need is to feel appreciated. "

H. Jackson Brown

Marriage Tip #25

In order to keep the spark alive and avoid "roommate syndrome," couples have to understand the notion of spending "time" together versus creating **"sacred"** time together. Spending time at social events, time with family and doing **"chores"** together does not count as sacred time. Instead, carve out special time to not only be intimate, but also ensure that you continue to share new experiences together such as hiking, exploring someplace new, or arranging a stay-cation in your own city.

Marriage Tip #26

Compliment your spouse every day! When is the last time you complimented your spouse? i.e. Said something nice to them about them being them... A compliment is a sign of acknowledgment and appreciation. Make an effort to affirm your spouse's value in life, and in love. Compliments are one of the most extraordinary components of social life. If given right they create so much positive energy that they make things happen almost as if by magic. They ease the atmosphere around two people and kindly dispose people to each other. **Of course, there is a way to give compliments. And, just as important, a way to receive compliments.** And everyone needs to know how to do both. Compliments derive from taking notice of praiseworthy situations and efforts. So they are also marks of both, awareness and consciousness. We need to cultivate awareness of the good developments that are all around us. Once praiseworthy situations are noticed, the awareness needs to be spoken. In other words, the compliment needs to be put forth into the world in spoken form. We deliver praise. People benefit from being the objects of compliments, but we also benefit being givers of them. Recipients benefit from knowing that we notice and learning that we value them. So compliments are powerful in motivating continued efforts. **People strive to do more of what brings praise from others.** Focusing on and noticing the good qualities in the world around us gives our moods a boost all by itself. Plus, it is a kind of **cognitive** training, a training of attention. In addition, compliments amplify positivity; they not only deliver positive effects to others, those effects bounce back on us, ramping up the positive atmosphere we breath. What compliments does your husband really need to hear from you? What compliments does your wife need to hear from you? What compliments do each of your children, individually, really need to hear from both of you?

Marriage Tip #27

Create a clear vision of your shared future together. Sit down, listen to each other and write out how you want your future as a couple to look. It's much easier to create your best relationship together if both people's needs are voiced, heard and supported by their partner. Get a vision board together of what you both would like to bring into your lives over the next year, next five years and even, the next ten years. Who would you like to meet? Where would you both like to go, together? **Ideas are the real power behind any husband / wife and any movement in their marriages.** There is no great husband / wife in history that has ever been great without an underlying idea that was the source of their greatness. **Most great husbands / wives draw strength, guidance, and vision from their ideas. And when they spread their ideas to their children, they spread their vision and give hope to their families based upon their families' acceptance of their ideas.** What new ideas will you and your spouse utilize to give to the rest of your team members as your families leaders? How will you influence your family to accept them? *Where there is no vision flowing from the dominant ideas in our heads about what we are ultimately doing as two people in the process of marriage then our families will continue to perish.*

Marriage Tip #28

Censor every impulse to blame or criticize your partner. Do everything you can to support your partner's well-being, and respect your partner as you would your best friend.

A strong marriage doesn't always have two strong people at the same time. It is a husband and wife who take turns being strong for each other in the moments when the other feels weak.

DrLaura.com

Marriage Tip #29

Schedule a regular date night because we need to date and court our mates. It's very important. Never stop dating or courting your spouse. Date night is sacred and special and should be on the same day of the week every week. One week the wife should suggest the date idea and the husband should come up with the date night plan for the opposite week. This encourages both the husband and wife to be invested in date night. Every week if possible, go out on a date just like you did before you were married. Select an activity where the two of you can interact, talk, and just be together enjoying each other's company (not a movie!). Even if you can't afford dinner and a movie (which we seldom can), spending some regular one-on-one time with your spouse is essential. Don't talk about bills, or schedules, or the kids. Daydream together about your future, or plan your dream vacation. End your date in the bedroom. Works like a charm! You will connect emotionally and often learn something new about each other – even after several years of being together. **Research by the Gottman Institute shows that many marriages end due to loss of intimacy and connection (especially 10 to 12 years in to the marriage).** Regular date nights are one of the best ways to help prevent the "silent drift apart" over time.

Marriage Tip #31

One of the most important factors in a good marriage is respect. When a husband shows love for his wife that motivates her to respect him more. When a wife shows more respect for her husband that motivates his love for her. This is a principle of marriage that is generally true across religious backgrounds and cultures. Of course, there are some exceptions where one spouse is not good-willed towards the other, or where one or both are so wounded, that it takes a very long time to rebuild the trust. But in general, most spouses are good-willed towards each other and want to please one another. We are just built and wired so differently as men and women that we often misunderstand and misinterpret the messages the other is sending. Men tend to think in the realm of respect. Women tend to think in the realm of love. Unfortunately – what men often do to be respectful, can feel unloving to their wives. And what wives often do to be loving, can feel disrespectful to their husbands. By learning to stretch and reach our spouse and meet his / her needs, we achieve God's glory. Let us be very clear, both husbands and wives need to be loved! But most husbands may feel inadequate to express to you just how important that respect is for them. A man's greatest need in this world is to be respected, and the person he desires that respect from the most is his wife. The trap that we've all been ensnared by is that they only deserve our respect when they earn it. Yes, you want your husband to make decisions that will ultimately garner your respect, but the truth is that your husband is a human being who has not yet arrived to a full manifestation of his divinity just yet. He is a human being who makes mistakes. This is the man that YOU have chosen to walk alongside you for the rest of your life, and to lead your family and he needs to be respected for that quality alone. When respect is given even when he doesn't deserve it, it will motivate him to earn it. That doesn't mean you pretend that his choices are good ones when they aren't. Things like that still need to be communicated, but you can flesh out your differences with respect. It makes all the difference in the world to him.

Maybe you should ask your husband straight up, **"What makes you feel respected by me?"** And then wait for his answer. Maybe respect isn't the habit in your marriage. Here is a small list that the wise men and women have given to us to help wives to be more successful in the **"respect"** area of their marriage:

* listen without interrupting your husband
* don't think for your husband
* don't use your "dumb guy" voice when repeating what your husband has that you don't agree with or that you think is stupid
* do not correct your husband's handling of the children or anything else in front of anyone. Do so in private.
* tell your husband what kind of physical intimacy you like – it makes him feel more at ease and more purposeful in pleasing you
* don't over-talk things with your husband — try to use short sentence and direct words. Your husband is a man and not one of your girlfriends.
* When a big decision comes up and your husband says he needs time to think about it let him think about it. If you tell him, **"Don't bother. I'll just do it my way,"** then what's the point of asking in the first place?
* When you tell your husband not now or not tonight, how about tomorrow (about any topic) then keep your word and re-arrange whatever you are doing to make sure you keep your word. This is super important that you keep your word in the marriage too!
* Find out what your husband takes as his most important responsibility and praise him for it... (being a great father, being a great provider, being a great husband, etc).
* Find out what your husband's love language is and surprise him with something spontaneous that's just for him.
* Flirt with him in public, at a party, where other people (especially his friends / co-workers) can see it.
* Offer your husband a back rub. Even if physical touch is not his love language most men carry a large burden (physically, spiritually, emotionally) on their shoulders and to offer up a back rub without being prompted is a wonderful release.

* If your husband comes to talk to you (about anything) put down the phone/tablet/computer with facebook / texting and give him your full attention. It's no different than when you want him to pause / turn off the TV when you want to talk to him.

* Let your husband know when he does things that make you happy. Most husband's biggest goal in marriage is to make their wives happy.

* Stop speaking "bad" about your husband to **anyone.**

* Seek your husband out if there is a "big" decision to be made about the home, children or finances, even if it is something he knows that he trusts you with and don't have an opinion about either way, please realize that he may see things from a different angle and give him the opportunity to affirm or to change his position.

Marriage Tip #32

Women tend to be more concerned about their marriages than men. They buy most of the books on marriage to try to improve them and initiate most marriage counseling. They often complain about their marriages to their closest friends and sometimes to anyone who will listen. And they also file for divorce twice as often as men. **Husbands… do you know how to make your wife feel loved? Below is a small list of ways to NOT make your wife feel special at all.**

"I hurt all the time because I feel alone and abandoned."
"My husband is no longer my friend."
"The only time he pays attention to me is when he wants sex."
"He is never there for me when I need him the most."
"When he hurts my feelings he doesn't apologize."
"He lives his life as if we weren't married; he rarely considers me."
"We're like ships passing in the night, he goes his way and I go mine."
"My husband has become a stranger to me, I don't even know who he is anymore."
"He doesn't show any interest in me or what I do."
"He would rather be with "the fellas, "the brothers" etc, etc than with me, his wife"

How to make your wife feel terrific, loved and truly special to you:
Use this list to learn what speaks "love" to her. It's likely very different from what speaks "love" to you. Your relationship can be strengthened by using this as a guideline —but keep in mind that these are only suggestions.

1. Lead your wife in prayer together.
2. Pray for your wife every day and make it a point to pray with her when she is troubled.
3. Communicate with your wife instead of talking at her or shutting her out emotionally from your life.

4. Talk to your wife respectfully without demeaning her or hurting her feelings.

5. Compliment your wife for the giftedness you see in her. Be specific.

6. Show interest in your wife's life. If she has friends that are trustworthy and honorable, give her time to be with them.

7. Do something active together to lift your wife's spirit —even if it's just taking a walk hand-in-hand.

8. Express to her that you need and value her.

9. Show enthusiasm for the things that she's excited about—let your actions show it.

10. Find something that makes you laugh together.

11. Put your arms around her when she needs comfort, holding her silently.

12. Surprise her by doing something you think she would want done before she asks.

13. Try not to make sudden changes without discussing them with her first.

14. Turn the TV down or off when she is trying to speak with you about something and face her directly.

15. Allow your wife to teach you things without being defensive.

16. When you feel you must correct her, be gentle —speak the truth in LOVE. Decide if you want your spouse to do something – or do something YOUR WAY... because once you try to correct them, you may find yourself doing it yourself.

17. Let go of the small stuff. We all have annoying habits and preferences that are different from our spouse's.

18. Show her that she matters more to you than any one you could be with, that threatens her security in your marriage.

19. Be a good listener. Show her you value what she says.

20. Plan a mini-honeymoon, where the two of you can spend quality time together.

21. Go shopping with her and don't sigh or look at what time it is even once.

22. Take her out to breakfast or make her breakfast (cleaning up afterward). That means you have to cook.

10 Things *to say* to your Husband
WHEN MARRIAGE IS HARD

1. What do you need from me right now?

2. How can I help you take some of the burden off today?

3. I'm sorry.

4. Thank you for_____.

5. I'm proud of you because_____.

6. Our kids are lucky to have a dad like you.

7. Please forgive me.

8. I love you because_____.

9. I'm going to make more of an effort to_____.

10. Thank you for being someone I can respect.

KathiLipp.com

Marriage Tip #34

Read through this marriage tip very slowly and carefully... A wise man taught me as I was getting ready to enter into the marriage process with Cecelia, **"You can't protect that which you cannot control."** Of course, I was young and very ignorant of how to go about approaching this wisdom set out to control Cecelia. I never even bothered to ask the brother, **"What do you mean by this statement? How can I accomplish this?"** My ignorant thought patterns and made my marriage so tense and simple situations became unnecessarily volatile. Many women are increasingly concerned about power and control in marital relationships. Women usually have good reason to be alarmed at the controlling behavior of their husbands and men who are being controlled by their wives do as well. We know from our work with marriages that situations exist where the wife thoroughly and skilfully dominates or controls the husband. The attempt of one spouse to control another is a short-sighted solution to marital conflict that backfires every time. We would be shocked at what both women and men put up with when married to a controlling spouse. Some of us don't know when our spouses are really trying to control us, or we are just engaging in paranoid thinking? Most controlling or dominating spouses have little comprehension of how their actions affect their spouses. As they become aware of their husband or wife's negative reactions to them, they typically justify their behaviors by explaining their intentions. You will often hear a controlling spouse, whether male or female, say things such as:

"I thought I was helping by pointing out things she could do better."

"I admit that I can be a little harsh in the way I say things, but that's just the way I am. He knew that when he married me. I never meant to make him feel badly about himself."

"If I didn't control the money, she'd spend us into the poor house. If I let her do what she wanted, our children would be wearing hand-me-downs."

"Isn't it fair for me to say what I think? I was only standing up for what I believe and I can't help it if that offends him."
"I think I have a right to have her take care of me and my needs rather than always running off to do any and everything her family wants from her. I wasn't controlling; I was trying to make my marriage work."

From their viewpoint, they did nothing wrong. However, their spouses feel anger, resentment, and sometimes bitterness because of the way they have been treated. Here are just some of the ways that some spouses go to the extreme in trying to control their spouse.

Some spouses *are extreme* in their efforts to *control what their spouse does, wears* and their personal dress code, what their spouse eats, *sees and sites their spouse visits on the Internet, their spouses practice of* religion, their spouses language, schedule and even their private prayers.

Some spouses even use their anger to control their spouse. They get very angry if their spouse makes any kind of mistake. They are constantly yelling and scolding their spouses. Some controlling spouses give their spouse the silent treatment for days at a time when they get mad at them. Though they probably never will hit or hurt their spouse physically, controlling spouses are generally very verbally abusive and tend to lecture their spouse like a little child. In their past and they still presently have anger issues and their spouses are afraid of their outbursts.

Some controlling spouses use *criticism and sarcasm,* which is a form of advanced anger, on their spouses. They are verbally critical and find ways to twist anything their spouse values into a weapon to control them. They try very hard to make their spouse feel that they are a bad person and that they are wrong and undeserving."

Some controlling spouses *act superior to their spouses.* They expect their spouse to do things and think the way they do. They sincerely believe that their way is not only better but the only way that this task or that task can be done. For the controlling spouse, their verbal abuse comes in the form of questioning everything their spouse does or says. Any opinion or knowledge that their spouse may have of a subject is dismissed as stupid or incorrect. The controlling spouse tends to act like the ultimate know-it-all and the rest of the world is inferior to them because their own self-esteem is in the toilet. Most controlling wives or husbands come across very charming and affable to the outside world, but at home they are totally different. All of their friends would be shocked if they really knew what he or she was really like.

Some controlling spouses control all the money in the home. They try to control their paycheck and their spouse's paycheck as well and then ultimately may want to give their spouse an allowance to spend from. Yet, they spend money freely with no regard to their families' ability to earn the money back. They force their spouse to cut coupons, shop sales, etc., and then write the check for the full amount. Force has no place in our marriages when the real need is for our acquisition of better skills and plenty of auditing... Some controlling spouses who bring in the income for the family solely feel the need to always make it clear that they have made all the money. It is not beneath a controlling spouse to even accuse their spouse of stealing from them.

Some controlling spouses try to dominate or embarrass their spouses: Some spouses still drink and become exceptionally mean, usually only to their spouse. They drink a lot and cause their spouses to create diversions to get them home before they launch into their spouse and eliminate any chance of a social life. Some controlling spouses even lie on their spouse. Their goal is very simple. They wish to isolate you from others so it will be just you... and them. They want to be in total control of whom you spend any time with or talk to. *They don't even want you around or spending* *time with your own blood* family or friends. Controlling spouse are overbearing and do not like their spouses to do anything without them.

Controlling spouses justify their negative behavior and blames their spouse for his / her behavior. They do not want their partner to make any major decisions yet won't help their spouse to make any decisions. Once any decision is made that they naturally don't agree with, then they will throw a tantrum like a 2-year-old. They ask their spouse if they can go out to eat when he knows they are low on money. Because their spouse doesn't want another angry encounter and outburst, they go. A week or two later when they don't have the money to pay bills they get angry anyway and blame their spouse for not managing the money well. In most cases, controlling spouses dominates while giving the illusion that their spouse is totally in control. They do this because they were totally dominated by someone when they were a young person. Hurt people, hurt people.

Controlling spouses dominate their spouse in sexual ways: They pout if their partner refuses sex, even for legitimate reasons such as a bad headache or an illness. They then blame their spouse for the lack of sex in the marriage relationship. The pressure to have sex is immense and yet the controlling spouse is very distant emotionally when it comes to sex. It could be anyone; they just need a body to satisfy their need. Controlling spouse will always leave a lingering threat that they will get back into porn if their spouse doesn't satisfy their need. Controlling spouses are notorious for withdrawing all emotional support. They withdraw all sexual relations, including simple things such as sitting near, kissing, etc., and not just intercourse. Sex with a controlling person is either their way on their twisted terms or nothing at all.

We don't need to try to excessively control our partners. Trying to control each other is one of the main sources of marital unhappiness. In a happy marriage, partners know they cannot excessively control each other. Learning not to control a partner can be a long process. Ask yourself: **"If I can only control my own behavior, what can I do to help the marriage?"** Then think of what you can change to make the problem better.

Did you recognize you or your spouse in anything that you just read?

Tips to stop the controller from exercising their inordinate control over you:

Seek refuge and protection in Almighty God.

Strive to find a good Student Minister or counseling service to talk with. They can help validate your feelings and make you feel stronger. They also can guide you in regards to possible ways you can make the relationship work by teaching you assertive skills. Your partner won't like it, but if they are at risk to lose their family, then many times they will begrudgingly change.

Confront the controller. They may make you feel like you are the crazy one or they may belittle you (they can do this with a look, with the silent treatment, with physical harm or with the use of words). When you confront them make sure you tell someone else what you are going to do so you have a safety plan in place. Controllers don't like being controlled and they can leave or get angry.

Work on your own self-esteem. Controllers are actually terrified of failure so they usually never admit when something is their fault. Rarely do they say they are sorry. Therefore, you end up feeling like everything is your fault. It's not. You are not the failure. If you can do the things that make you feel good about yourself, you can begin to be more assertive and less likely to be used as a doormat.

Invest in yourself again by reaching out to family and friends. This is going to help you understand that you are still a loveable wonderful person and to help you feel supported.

Decide on a plan to work out the relationship or leave. The most important thing about your plan is that it has a limited time, so you have control. If you are thinking of changing your controller, forget it. The controller is the only one who can control themselves and their behavior. If a controller does not change their controlling behavior, they usually worsen with time instead of growing mellower.

Relationships take negotiation skills and the ability to be flexible. A controlling person lacks both of these very important skills. If they are able to see what they are doing to their spouse, they can make changes. However, for them to be able to evaluate and understand how it feels to be controlled is very difficult. Enter these relationships at your own risk and take control of your own needs if you have to get out. We are true marriage advocates, but living with a true "controller" is not something we advocate. You can have control or you can have connection with your partner, but you can't have both. Pursue connection!

"Controllers, abusers and manipulative people don't question themselves. They don't ask themselves if the problem is them. They always say the problem is someone else."
-Darlene Ouimet

Marriage Tip #35

It is the responsibility of both the father and the mother to teach your children the Bible and the Holy Qur'an. Stop thinking it is the responsibility of one parent alone. We both have to teach our children values, etiquettes and morals. Wouldn't you just hate it, if one day, when your children got older, they said that all you ever taught them is how to sit in front of the TV for hours? Or they said, you only taught them how to roam around in shopping centers for hours on end. Always strive hard to save your progeny.

Marriage Tip #36

Couples often lose each other because of their busy lives: work, children, computers, and separate male/female activities. A healthy marriage is one that has a mix of individual, family, and couple time. The amount of each may be different for each couple, but the mix is necessary to keep a functional marriage.

Stop trying to make your spouse be more like you. That won't make your marriage work. Support each other as you are.

Marriage Tip #37

Our brains are the only organ in the human body which do not self-regulate, but need to be in connection with another brain for healing. Sit face-to-face and gaze into your spouse's eyes in order to allow the limbic system to relax. This will bring you closer and create the deepest sort of intimacy. A woman needs her partner to spend time giving her his full attention and looking directly into her eyes. When she receives this, she can easily get in touch with her feelings of love for her husband and becomes much more receptive to his needs. This is how intimacy can be fulfilling for both people ... magical even! Intimacy = In to Me See. The closer you and your spouse get, the more of YOU they will see and love. Get intimate with your spouse & allow them to get to know you! Intimacy is not negotiable in a healthy, long-term partnership. Touch is one of the most nurturing forces in the universe. If you're iffy on your partner touching you, it's important to explore what's going on and work on it. Communication also builds intimacy. Intimacy is all about connection, openness, and vulnerability, so fostering healthy, consistent communication is the bridge to regular intimacy. This means hearing and listening to your partner and truly wanting to understand what they're saying.

Marriage Tip #38

When you first see each other at the end of your respective days, before you do anything else, hold each other without speaking for at least five seconds. Let Luther Vandross or your favorite R & B Singer do the talking for you. This will help to remind you both that you are a source of pleasure and comfort. It's simple, it's easy to do, and it will make a world of difference.

Marriage Tip #39

Preface important communication with a simple yet effective introduction. Try: **"Honey, I'm confused about your response to my plans for a weekend trip with my friends. When would be a good time to talk further?"** Couples have found that prefacing their remarks like this with their spouse encourages a better, more accommodating reaction from their partner. Most marriages could stand a whole lot more encouragement. This is very important for wives to understand. **Nothing is so common as unsuccessful men with talent. They lack only determination.**

Marriage Tip #40

On those ever-important date nights, remember to be a wife first and a critic second. **Every time you open your mouth to complain about something — whether it's the food, the service, the movie, the weather, whatever — some part of your partner feels he's failing because you aren't having a great time.** Even listening to words of complaint for as little as 30 minutes strips away neurons in the hippocampus area of our brains and turns our spouse's brain to 'mush'. Men are happiest when they can please their woman! Save the full critique for your girlfriends and in meantime, let him see the best in you. Why don't you try sharing with your spouse how you would like things to be rather than complaining about how things are?

Stop Complaining

Go 24 hours without complaining. (Not even once.) Then watch how your life starts changing!

Marriage Tip #41

Lean in. When it gets hard in a relationship, our tendency is to protect ourselves, to retreat, to **"lean out."** Leaning out when your partner reaches out creates distance and dissonance. If instead you **"lean in"** to the uncomfortable feelings, to the unknown and your own vulnerability, and meet your partner, you can actually strengthen your relationship through the struggles you face together. Reassure your spouse of your love and that your love will be there regardless of the challenge. Replace the seven deadly habits in marriages with the seven caring habits. Putting them into practice will take effort.

The seven deadly habits in marriages are criticizing, blaming, complaining, nagging, threatening, punishing, and bribing.

The seven caring habits in marriage include supporting, encouraging, listening, accepting, trusting, respecting, and negotiating your differences.

Marriage Tip #42

Accept your partner exactly as they are today. Don't try to change him / her. Instead...

MARRIAGE TIPS:
* Always greet each other with a smile.
* Make time for each other.
* Share with each other what you're thankful for.
* Say things that build up each other in private and public.
* Use kind words – not rude words.
* Have a financial plan and work together toward the goal.
* Be the first one to forgive. No egos allowed in a marriage.
* Pray for one another, pray together.
* Set a regular date night at least once a month.
* Never be afraid to ask for help.

Marriage Tip #43

When your partner tells you something (about you) that is bothering them, reflect back what they are saying. When we "mirror", this helps us not feel as defensive and allows us the opportunity to better understand what they are trying to communicate.

Marriage Tip #44

The best way to strengthen a marriage is to support and assist each other in being the best you can be. A strong marriage is one in which both people understand that the other person needs to have outside interests and activities which help them to feel happy and fulfilled. A strong marriage is one where both people understand that it is more important to be happy than it is to be right.

Marriage Tip #45

Have you lost that loving feeling? Step 1: Write down 10 qualities you loved about your partner when you first met and read it to each other. Step 2: Brainstorm a list of 10 fun things you did together when you first met; do one date per week and enjoy bringing back that loving feeling!

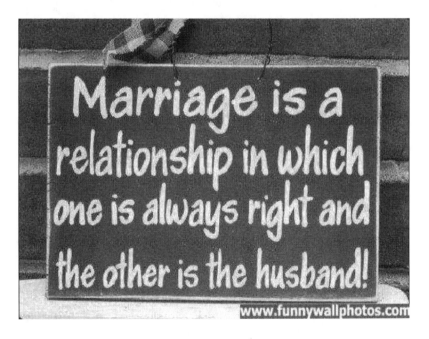

Marriage Tip #46

You're entitled to the occasional bad mood. You're not entitled to make your partner your personal and perpetual whipping boy or girl.

Marriage Tip #47

A strong marriage is a partnership in trust. Trust your partner in everything, including purchases and financial decisions, and to bring up things with you that need a joint decision. If you can't do that, the two of you have a problem.

Marriage Tip #48

Always remember that life is long. In the heat of the moment, what feels super-important will likely fade in importance as time goes by. Before you react by yelling, tossing insults or unkind words, remember that **"This, too, shall pass"**. In fact, recent studies have shown that even the unhappiest of couples report being very happy five years later. So don't let one unfortunate incident, difficult argument or challenging moment destroy your lifetime of happiness.

Marriage Tip #49

Your spouse is not your enemy. That is all...

Marriage Tip #50

Use character-related words that honor your spouse for such qualities as patience, helpfulness, courage, or kindness. Create regular opportunities for fun, laughter, and positive experiences. Figure out what communicates love to each other and do that. Be observant and thoughtful with little things and even do chores that the other dislikes. Consciously doing what opens and softens your spouse's heart will benefit you both in the long-run and keep your marriage happier.

Marriage Tip #51

If it is possible, take a day off from work for your spouse and work on each other. If you can't do that, and they are off, make sure they can enjoy their time off. When you are able to reconnect with them later on, ask them questions to help them explore their day. Be happy for your partner and their successes! Get back into your partner!

Marriage Tip #52

Guard your heart. – The grass is not greener on the other side. Do not believe the lie that with a slimmer figure, a higher salary, a faster car, or a bigger house, you will be a happier person. The world is full of things and people that will serve as reminders that you don't have the best of the best, but it's simply not true. Live the life you've been blessed with, and BE THANKFUL. Guard your heart from things and people that will try to convince you that your life or your spouse is not good enough. There will always be bigger, faster, stronger, or shinier – but you'll never be satisfied with more until you're fulfilled with what you have now.

Marriage Tip #53

When you board an airplane, the flight attendants are required to go over emergency preparedness prior to takeoff. When explaining the part about how to operate the oxygen mask, passengers are instructed to first put the mask on themselves before putting it on their small child. Is that because they think you are more important than your kids? Absolutely not. **But you cannot effectively help your child if you can't breathe yourself.** The same holds true with marriage and parenting. You cannot effectively parent your children if your marriage is falling apart. The order is Almighty God, your spouse and then your children...in that order. – I know this isn't a popular philosophy, but hear us out. God has to come first in our lives no matter what. But regardless of your belief system, your spouse should come before your children. No spouse in their right mind would ask you to put the children aside to serve their every need while neglecting them. That's not what this means. There will come a time when the children will leave the house to pursue their dreams as adults. If we have not cultivated a lasting relationship with our spouses, we will have both empty nests and empty hearts.

The Empty Nest

How to Survive –
or even Thrive!

Marriage Tip #54

Forgive. – No one is perfect. Everyone makes mistakes so drop your grudges against your spouse as fast as humanly possible. Have you ever noticed that we talk about grudges like they're helpless infants who need our care? **We "nurse" grudges and "hold" grudges and "suckle them at our bosoms like little newborn infants who need nutrition."** All are common and accurate idioms to describe what it takes to carry a tiny baby insult to a full grown manbeast that has its own hair and a mortgage. Despite the coddling, nursing, and suckling it takes to keep them alive, there is nothing that will rot your soul from the inside out more thoroughly than a grudge.

Even when they're completely justified, those little pockets of resentment that we secretly harbor for a rainy day are as poisonous as a ham sandwich on wheat bread, and the first thing they murder is our own peace of mind. The second thing they murder is our marriage relationship.

As a child, our grudges are managed by the people around us. If we're not bleeding or emotionally traumatized, our parents probably don't care that the universe hasn't treated us fairly, which is why petty grudges get dropped during commercial breaks. As a grownup, the grudge police don't exist. Unless we're dealing with grudges that come from actual crimes, in which case go ahead and use the real-world police as your grudge police.

Once we're permanently sharing a bed with someone, there's nowhere to hide from our hurt feelings. That is, unless you take this shortcut:
Be the first to apologize. Even when you're right and you both know it. Obviously, this advice doesn't work for people in toxic relationships. If you're with someone who is an unrepentantly bad person who hurts you for fun, you're probably better off cutting your losses and call it a day. But most of us aren't in toxic

relationships; we're in perfectly fine marriages comprised of two well-meaning humans who don't know what to do with themselves when they get their feelings hurt. Nurturing hurt feelings is as useful as nurturing a rock. Give them an hour to stew, cry a little bit, then we should drop them. After all, is teaching your husband or wife a lesson more important than whatever else you could be doing? If your spouse hasn't lied, cheated, abused, or otherwise wronged you in a way that would warrant a Lifetime storyline, there's a 99 percent chance that the grudge you're holding isn't worth 30 more minutes of your time. Especially if you'd be embarrassed to explain the fight to a third party, if you could even remember what you were mad about in the first place. If being right makes you happier than being happy, then good luck with the rest of your life. If you make forgiveness a habit – for everything from major mistakes to little annoyances you will keep resentment from growing.

Marriage Tip #55

Over-communicate. – Many spouses have the bad habit of not speaking our feelings. We have also played the standard **"You should know why I'm mad"** game, and that's just downright unfair. Men and women are not wired like each other and because of that we don't always know that we've been insensitive. We think that our spouse should be able to look at us and tell we have offended them. Some spouses want their spouse to pry every feeling or sentiment out of them. Again, this is not fair to them. Strive hard to be a mature adult and communicate how you feel to your spouse.

Marriage Tip #56

What about when we need space from each other? Well here are 5 marriage tips when, **"we need our space from each other"**

1. Text each other.
When you're angry it's hard to have a rational conversation. But texting is a chance to still be polite to each other, explain how you feel and cry without feeling eyes on you. It's a safe environment that keeps the connection alive, while actively working towards solving the issue.

2. Establish equal ground
Arguments lead to blame. It's so easy to want to blame each other. Please don't do this. Accept that if you're both arguing, then you both have some fault in the matter. All arguments are simply a misstep in communication. If we had no faults of our own, we would not take so much pleasure in noticing those of our spouses. So if you can both acknowledge that you both simply feel disconnected from each other, blame leaves the conversation.

3. Agree to switch course
There's a moment right before you decide to quit and retreat to your space, before you clam up and the negatively begins to flow from everything you do. In that moment, you both have to decide that you both will handle stress and anger better. Come up with a plan. If you're frustrated, the last thing you want to do is direct it at each other.

4. Let it out!
Everyone gets angry and it's a valid emotion to have. So while we are not saying not to get mad or frustrated, we are saying you should strategically let it out so that it isn't used selfishly. Directing your anger or stress from the day or the task in front of you is selfish because it only caters to how you feel. Scream out to help

you release your stress. Then turn to your partner and smile or laugh or kiss them or hug them.

5. Commit

If these little hacks feel weird to you, good! It's the weird and uncomfortable things we feel, that are often the things we need to prioritize. Learning to love your partner better is definitely a priority. Things are so much more fun and less stressful now that we've done this ourselves. We've chosen to be together for the rest of our lives, so we better have a good plan for seeing it through. We like to think of loving someone as a decision. We choose to love every day, because there's just too much other stuff to worry about in this life. Running your life is enough. The choice to love is easy, executing can be more taxing some days, but as always it's the only choice and act that we never think twice about. **Research** finds that couples that split household duties, including cooking, cleaning and child rearing, enjoy more sex and are happier than couples where the woman tackles **"feminine"** tasks and the man tackles **"manly"** tasks. Do everything as a team. Raise the children together. The concept of teamwork should be instrumental in our marriage.

Marriage Tip #57

Never say the "D Word" – Have you figured out the difference between you, your husband, all your divorced friends, relatives, co-workers, neighbors, and fellow humans? We can tell you! Are you ready? There is no difference. None!

With the taste of wedding cake barely off their lips, divorce is the last thought -- or word -- on newlyweds' minds. But as the honeymoon period wanes, and day-to-day difficulties crop up, the word can come up frequently during arguments for some couples. There's no anniversary where the doctor gives you a divorce vaccine that makes you immune from breaking up. Just because you've been married so many years that your anniversary ends in a "0" or a "5," or your grandchildren throw you a party, doesn't mean you've passed the point where the little kingdom you've built won't crumble to a million little pieces if you sneeze hard enough. All I've figured out so far is that we've been lucky, because neither one of us has followed through with a case of the **"What ifs?"** Nowadays we are seeing people get divorced after reaching a 20, 20, 40, 50 and even 60 year milestone.

Some of the most miserable people we've ever met were languishing in coffins disguised as marriages. Keeping a good thing going is only worth it when it's a good thing to begin with. If you're gonna say it, you better mean it. **Plain and simple, threatening divorce is not fighting fair.** Sometimes we are hurting so deeply from our spouse's words or actions, and we want to hurt our spouses back, so we throw it out there at our spouses. Just don't go there. Some people pull that out much too early, and much too often in a relationship. It raises a whole level of **anxiety** [in the person hearing it]. Don't use the D word! You need all your energy to find the solution to a problem and work it out. If you are even giving any consideration to a divorce, you lessen your ability to solve the problem. Yes, some situations are deal breakers, such as **addiction**, adultery, or abuse. But when the problem is less severe, create a "ledger of life." Get out a piece of paper and write down everything that you love about your spouse. Eventually, you and your spouse will begin to shift gears and begin to focus on what is right, not what's wrong.

Marriage Tip #58

Learn your spouse's love language. Everyone has a love language. The way you perceive love is often different from the way your spouse perceives love. Do they like words of affirmation, or do they respond better when you give them gifts? Whatever your spouse's love language is – learn it and USE IT. Please go here for more information: www.5lovelanguages.com

Marriage Tip #59

Never talk negatively about your spouse. If you're going through a difficult time in your marriage and you need advice, see a counselor. Family counseling is a great tool, but try to remember that your family members and friends are not the most objective people to give advice. The argument they are hearing is one-sided and they often build up negative feelings toward your spouse, which usually doesn't subside once you and your spouse have gotten past it. Protect his image with those that you're close with and seek help from those that can actually be objective. News flash! Most mothers and fathers cannot be objective!

Honoring your marriage means showing respect to your spouse at all times in all situations. Don't talk badly about your spouse to your friends and don't tolerate any "friends" who talk badly about your spouse.

Marriage Tip #60

Choose to love. — There are times in a marriage that you may wake up and not feel in love anymore. Choose to love anyway. There are times when you may not be attracted to your spouse anymore. Choose to love anyway. Marriage is a commitment. In sickness and health, in good times and in bad. Those vows are sacred. They don't say **"if you have bad times"**. They say "in good times AND in bad", implying that there **will** be bad times. It's inevitable. So choose to love anyway. Your spouse is worth it.

Marriage Tip #61

Compliments complement. Couples who regularly give each other "affective affirmation" — meaning "compliments, help and support, encouragement and subtle nonsexual rewards, such as hand holding" — are the happiest. A key finding in marriages is that **"men crave affective affirmation more than women, because women typically get it from people other than their husbands."** A small compliment can go much further than you would ever guess. Don't forget to compliment your spouse when one is deserved. You never know when they could really use a few uplifting words to help transform their day or make their week better.

Compliments really *do* matter in a relationship—especially to people who tend to process things WITH THEIR HEART instead of their head or gut.

Marriage Tip #62

It's no surprise that when it comes to marriage, money consistently ranks as one of the top stressors that's ruined a fair share of relationships. We don't know if you know this but too much money can cause just as much dysfunction as having too little. Make it a practice to never argue about money because when the argument is over you are still broke.

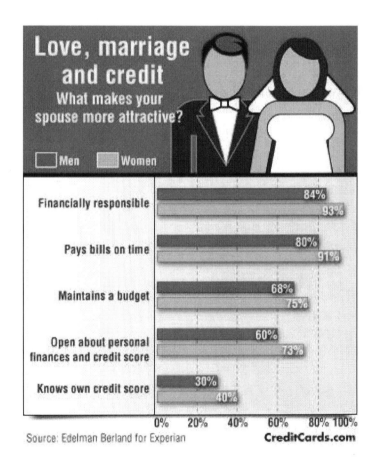

Love, marriage and credit
What makes your spouse more attractive?

☐ Men   ☐ Women

	Men	Women
Financially responsible	84%	93%
Pays bills on time	80%	91%
Maintains a budget	68%	75%
Open about personal finances and credit score	60%	73%
Knows own credit score	30%	40%

0% 20% 40% 60% 80% 100%

Source: Edelman Berland for Experian   **CreditCards.com**

Marriage Tip #63

It's a fact— Everyone is ignorant in some way or another and in marriages, our ignorance of so much and so many things is our deepest secret that we would hate for our spouse to discover about us. Ignorance is is one of the scariest things out there, because those of us who are most ignorant are also the ones who often don't know it or don't want to admit it. We should refrain from thinking we know everything that there is to know about our partners.

One of the best ways to overcome ignorance is to ask questions. One great way to explore your partner is to ask them open ended questions. The point here is that you talk, laugh, dream and learn more about each other. Some questions are silly while others really get you thinking about some possible big life decisions. Either way, pull these out on your next date night or after the children go to bed and spend time connecting with your spouse.

Would you rather stay in or go out for a date night?
Would you rather play a board game or watch a movie with me?
Would you rather be a movie star or a famous musician?
Would you rather go into the past and meet your ancestors or go into the future and meet your great-great grandchildren?
Would you rather spend the next year exempt from all taxes or have one month paid vacation?
Would you rather always speak your mind or never speak again?
Would you rather put a stop to war or end world hunger?
Would you rather give or get bad advice?
Would you rather lose your keys or your cell phone?
Would you rather always be gossiped about or never talked about?
Would you rather fail or never try?
Would you rather work in a group or work alone?
Would you rather be stuck on an island alone or with someone who talks incessantly?
Would you rather have more money or more time?

Would you rather have a cook or a maid?
Would you rather hear the good news or the bad news first?
Would you rather be your own boss or work for someone else?
Would you rather have nosy neighbors or noisy neighbors?
Would you rather have mind blowing sex once a month or mediocre sex once a week?
Would you rather be a little late or way too early?
Would you rather have an unlimited gift certificate to a restaurant or a clothing store?
Would you rather have many good friends or one very best friend?
Would you rather live in Antarctica or the Sahara Desert?
Would you rather be fluent in all languages or be a master of every musical instrument?
Would you rather fight all the time but have great make up sex or never fight and have mediocre sex?

Marriage Tip #64

"Learn How to Touch Your Wife in Ways That Have Nothing to do With Sex, But Rather, Everything to do with Comfort, Understanding and Protection."

Marriage Tip #65

Stay on your toes - Couples who believe they are in a relationship rut or feeling bored, are less happy over time. So escape the rut by mixing things up. **"The changes can be small, but they have to upset the routine enough to make both of you sit up and take notice."** Couples should keep on doing new things together, after they get into the process of marriage. Novelty drives up the dopamine system in the brain and can help to sustain feelings of love.

Marriage Tip #66

Marriage is like a credit card. Both couples have to work at sustaining their positive illusions about their significant other. When you begin to feel irritated at your partner, instead of reviewing everything you don't like, turn your thoughts to all the good things about him or her. Newlyweds automatically know how to speak to the positive and make each other feel special and valued. But the more enduring the marriage, the more you'll find yourself noticing and speaking to what you don't like. No one can survive in a marriage, at least not happily, if they feel more judged than admired. Relationships, like the economy, run on credit. In relationships we give "credit", or express gratitude, for the things your partner does that make your life easier and the things we often take for granted. We also advance credit to our spouse by assuming that they have good intentions and would like to step up to the plate, rather than assuming that we need to ride herd on them in order to get what we need.

Marriage Tip #67

Look for the soft emotion - Always strive to look for the soft emotion that lies beneath the hard one. Strive hard to respond to the soft emotion — the fear, anxiety or embarrassment that is hiding behind the anger or accusation — rather than to the hard one. It helps in all sorts of relationships, not just marriage.

Marriage Tip #68

The effect of our words in marriage - Just like a book, a marriage is full of words. What words are included will determine if it is a book of love. It's not only the words the couple uses that make a difference, friends, family and a good few others will throw theirs into the ring, as well. Our words help *to give our spouse's back their self-respect, belief in ourselves, the support we need to make crazy leaps of faith, and it also our spouse's words that provide the calming balm that restore us when we land on the ground.*

The power of words:

Life and death are in the power of words. We can help bring out the best in our spouses or we can help to destroy them, just with our words. Words are powers that no spouse should ever want to to misuse again.

Words change our behavior. In the UK documentary series 'The Young Ones' researchers exposed one group of university students to words about aging (i.e., old, infirm, hobble, wizened, geriatric), and another group to words around youth (i.e., skip, joy, jump, fun, young, energy) for just 10 minutes. Those exposed to the aged related words ambled from the room more slowly than when they had arrived, some were stooped and sad. Meanwhile those exposed to the youth related words walked faster or ran from the room, one even skipped and most were smiling.

Words affect our intelligence. Science is uncovering some very interesting understandings about words, for instance: exposure to a word can affect our actions, our feelings, our thinking and even our intelligence! This is especially true with the words we use to speak with our own children.

The words we say to our spouse's influence who they become. If exposure to one little word influences people then we have to keep in mind constantly just what influence our words have on who our spouses becomes. Some days we will have to choose our words carefully!

The words we say to others about our spouse will influence who they become – especially if we say those words in front of them. What your spouse hears you say about them builds their picture of themselves. Make sure your children understand this little gem as they become adults who will also seek marriage one day. Knowing this one little fact may stop them from destroying their future spouses.

Every single day we are influencing ourselves with the words we tell ourselves about ourselves. All those nasty little things we say to ourselves gain a foothold and bear sour fruit. Learning to speak nicely to ourselves grows much tastier fruit and everyone benefits.

Every single day we influence others with our words. This is often hard for us to remember. Sometimes we are quick to point out faults and much slower to find the good in the members of our own family. Some of us are professional fault finders. We have to send ourselves daily reminders to speak more kindly!

Words come with emotions attached. Do you have a stack of oft used words that regularly appear in your speech and reveal your issues? Have you struggled with fear and anxiety so your speech tends to be littered with words like "afraid", "fear", "Oh no!", and "That's terrible". Most situations don't call for such emotionally laden words.

10. Do you know that you and your spouse could see your situation very differently just by changing the words we both use. It isn't what happens to us that matters, it is how we think and speak about what happens that gives it power over us or us over it.

Words are powerful little things, aren't they? Our thoughts, actions, emotions, and even our brains can be affected by them. In marriage it is important that we remember the 'power' of words, and chose them wisely.

Words Can Hurt or Heal

What Did Yours Do Today?

Marriage Tip #69

Living with unmet sexual needs can lead to intense feelings of rejection...Don't wait for the mood to strike before you will reach for your spouse in a sexual manner. Many spouses do not bring the right attitude towards sexual relations with our spouse. There is nothing quite like trying to have sex with a person who doesn't want to have sex with you. We don't always have to expect to be overcome by desire before deciding to have sex with our spouse. Sexual stimulation of the genitals stimulates the dopamine system to sustain feelings of romantic love. With orgasm, one gets a flood of oxytocin and vasopressin, neurochemicals that give you feelings of attachment for your partner. That's not to mention that seminal fluid is a good antidepressant, full of chemicals that lift optimism. Be mindful husbands, that your wife wants to experience a "high" from sexual activity with you as much as you do. If you get yours while she rarely if ever gets to experience that high with and from you... she will grow weary of any sexual experience with you. Don't be a selfish lover!

90
The number of calories you can torch during a 30-minute sexual experience between couples, inclusive of foreplay, according to researchers from the University of Quebec. That's just about equivalent to a 13-minute jog! Your pelvic floor muscles – which play a role in incontinence when you're older – as well as your back, butt and thigh muscles can get a good workout too.

84
The number of 30-minute **sex sessions** it will take you to burn enough calories to lose a kilo.

5.6
According to the same study from the University of Quebec, the mean intensity of sex for wives is 5.6 METS (metabolic equivalent tasks – a measure of physical intensity). That's approximately the effort required to cycle or play doubles tennis.

10 years

You can shave a decade off your appearance if you have sex four times a week or more. Researchers at Royal Edinburgh Hospital attribute this to improved circulation, endorphin release and fat burning effects caused by sex.

30%

Having sex more than once a week can give you a whopping 30 per cent increase in levels of Immunoglobulin A (IgA) – an antibody that protects you against bacteria and viruses. Wilkes University researchers say that this boost to your immune system can help ward off common ailments like colds and flu.

50%

Prone to getting migraines? Grab your husband for a quickie! According to studies done by researchers from the University of Münster and Southern Illinois University, around half of couples who suffer from migraines felt better after sex. Apparently, the hormones produced during orgasm – oxytocin and endorphins – alleviate headaches naturally.

2 days

Besides headaches, sex can also relieve other forms of pain for up to two days, such as menstrual cramp, chronic back and leg pain, says Barry R Komisaruk, a psychology professor at Rutgers University. He also asserts that self-stimulation of the front wall of the vagina (where the G-spot is located) can produce a powerful anagelsic effect, thereby increasing pain tolerance by as much as 50 percent.

1 in 6

Sex is great for the sleepless. A study conducted by UK bodycare brand Sanctuary Spa found that one in six wives experience longer and deeper sleep after sex.

7 to 8 years

Wives who professed **enjoying their sex lives** were found to have lived seven to eight years longer than those who didn't, according to a Duke University study that was conducted over a period of 25 years. Researchers, however, said that longevity does depend on other factors too, like health, intelligence and activities that the wives engaged in.

2 weeks

In a study published in Biological Psychology, researchers from University of the West of Scotland say wives respond better to stressful situations when they have had intercourse at least once in the previous two weeks, compared with those who abstained or engaged in other sexual activities. The former were less uptight about speaking in public and doing verbal arithmetic due to the stress-busting hormones – endorphins and oxytocin – the body releases during sex.

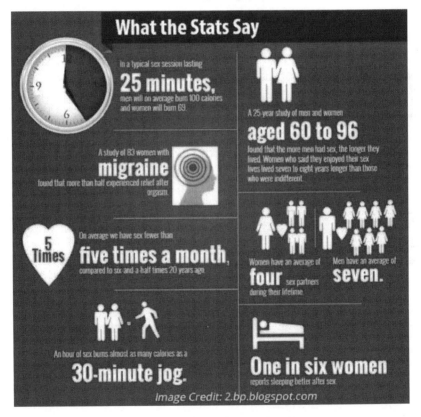

Image Credit: 2.bp.blogspot.com

Marriage Tip #70

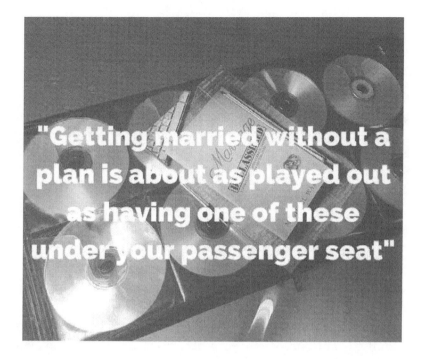

"Getting married without a plan is about as played out as having one of these under your passenger seat"

Marriage Tip #71

Sometimes love, is only love and that's perfect - There is something absolutely divine in the ability to put someone else in your heart and to think of them first. Many times we demand that love be something more... And what happens is, the utter grandeur and magnificence of what love actually is gets overshadowed by this disappointment that it's not the way we fantasized it should be.

Marriage Tip #72

Many marriages have suffered because one or both members of the couple have a sense of superiority. This means that they have had a feeling of entitlement that allows them to ignore mundane maintenance, leaving them free for pursuits that merit their interest like their careers or focusing on their tennis serve for example. Basically, they do what they want to do in the relationship while you do what you have to do. This is inequity that would infuriate anyone...

Marriage Tip #73

Love by itself is never enough to have a relationship work. The divorce courts are full of people who love each other. For example, what good is someone's love for you if the person treats you poorly? To have a relationship be great, you need more than love. You need the experience of love. If you want your relationship with your spouse to be great, you need to make sure they feel loved. When the experience of love is present, you are happy and alive. You feel good about yourself. You are positive, confident, and creative. The wise men and women have shared, **"Love is the most creative force in the universe"**. When we truly love we can build a lasting relationship with each other. People who truly love each other are dutiful to each other because they understand that love assigns its bearer a duty. We all have duties to one another. We should do our duty out of love for one another and our love for our spouse's Creator. Ultimately, this is the happiness that we seek. This is what we want in our relationships and in our lives. So what creates the experience of love? It is created by giving acceptance and appreciation.

Marriage Tip #74

Be willing to do more than your part. – You know it's never 50-50 in a great relationship at any given moment. It's always 75-25, or 60-40. Someone falls in love first. Someone gives a little more. Someone works very hard to keep things rolling smoothly when times get tough; someone else sails along for the ride for a while. And it flip-flops back and forth, depending on whose soul is stronger at the moment.

Marriage Tip #75

Think of Your Marriage Like a Business - Remember in The Godfather when Sonny and Michael discuss murdering people as business decisions? **"It's not personal, it's business,"** they said, before killing a cop and a mob boss, inciting a mafia war. Preserving a marriage feels like that sometimes, minus the homicide. Sure, you could act on your raw emotions every time you get your feelings hurt, you could call it quits when things aren't fun anymore, you could entertain the idea of meeting someone who **"gets you"** better -- but you do all of those things at the risk of throwing away your business. And by **"business"** we mean the partnership you agreed to at the altar. The one that's probably going to keep you **wealthier than your divorced and single friends**, the one that's going to keep you company when your children are grown and secretly grossed out by your neck flaps. The next time you and your husband or wife have a fight and you think about giving up, ask yourself this: **"After all we've been through, do I ever want to share a toilet with a whole new person?"** Stop and think if it will be a big deal in a few days, weeks, months, or years before you pick a fight about it.

Marriage Tip #76

Since some spouses have grown up being told to shut up then they continue these patterns as a grown adult. They do not express their feelings (for fear of getting hurt). This often leaves their partner very unsettled, thinking **"I don't know what is going on with him/her"**. It creates doubt about the strength of the relationship. A partner who clams up will avoid conflict at all cost. Their partner can feel very lonely, separated, confused and disconnected.

Here are some examples of a communicating pattern that avoids conflict and prefers to clam up and withdraw.

- OK
- I don't mind
- I don't care
- Your choice
- You do whatever you want
- If this is what you want
- I don't want to talk about it (in difficult situations)

- There is no point

- I have no desire to share my feelings

If you see yourself in these examples, seek help! Self-help and self-awareness are very successful tools to create change, but these communication styles are subconscious and most people are not aware of them at all. You can, over a long time, change this pattern, and hopefully your partner will stay until you finish the process, but with help, you will get there faster and in a very efficient way. You should definitely get audited.

Once bitten by a snake, he is scared all his life at the mere sight of a rope.

A person who goes into a shell and clams up is very much in the dark. They walk around fearing everything that resembles pain and this can take a lot of the passion out of a relationship or marriage.

Notice the way you communicate with your partner. Do you take the offensive, or the defensive? Are you always on guard or do you withdraw and clam up completely? With help, any relationship can be improved and turned into a positive one.

Marriage Tip #77

"WE CAN WORK IT OUT." - Notice the word "we" versus "I." Numerous studies have found a link between marital happiness and how often couples refer to themselves as "we." That's because seeing yourself as a team makes you more likely to cope well with the day-to-day problems that are inevitable in any long-term relationship. What's more, "we" lends a spirit of cooperation to your discussions -- and that not only results in fewer disagreements, but also arguments that get resolved more quickly. If you are having real, serious challenges to your marriage, know that another new baby is not the answer to the issues that you and your spouse face in the marriage. Let's get some strong, passionate communication going between you two in the living or the dining room and not necessarily the bedroom...

Marriage Tip #78

"I hear what you're saying." - If Cecelia and I, had a penny for each time we've heard a couple complain, **"My partner never listens,"** We would be very wealthy! We humans have a primal need to feel, both, heard and understood; this is especially true in relationships. When you don't feel heard and understood, you both struggle to feel important, valued, or connected to one another. Notice that this phrase doesn't necessarily mean that you agree with what's being said. But, it does send a critical message that you're listening with an open mind. And when that happens, your significant other is far more likely to share his or her innermost thoughts and feelings with you, which, naturally, tightens your bond.

Marriage Tip #79

"I'm crazy about you!!" - Most of us think nice thoughts about our mates all the time, but all too often, we keep them to ourselves. The truth is, our significant others need to hear (again and again) how smart, charming, attractive and wonderful we think they are. In fact, constant reminders from the person whose opinion they value most (that'd be you!) keep your partner's self-confidence soaring, spirits high, and his / her connection to you closer than ever.

Marriage Tip #80

"WOW, THANK YOU!" - In the happiest relationships, couples make a point of acknowledging all the little things -- from his clearing the table or taking the kids to the park, to her picking up the dry cleaning or making your favorite meal. But the closest couples add an exclamation to their thanks. Adding a "Wow!" is like underlining your thanks or putting it in bold type, so you know for sure that your partner feels loved and appreciated. In fact, according to behavioral science expert, an exclamation actually registers differently on the cochlea -- the part of the inner ear that receives and analyzes sound -- so your partner literally perks up, listens, and better hears what's being said. This is very important because we tend to remember the good things that we do, but forget the good things that our spouses do...

Marriage Tip #81

Skip the weather report and dive into a truly interesting conversation together. Good conversation with our spouses is as stimulating as black coffee, and just as hard to sleep after....
Do you and your honey chit chat about the weather and random details of your work day ... or do you make time to really talk?
A study in **Psychological Science** claims that people are happier when they spend more time discussing meaningful topics than engaging in small talk.
Seventy-nine college students had their conversations recorded and analyzed by researchers, who distinguished between chit-chat about the food or the weather from discussions about philosophy, education, or religion. Subjects who reported the greatest amount of satisfaction spent only 10 percent of their **conversation** on small talk, while the unhappiest subjects kept 28.3 percent of their talking time in the shallow end.
Granted, the researchers have yet to conclude whether people are happy because they can talk deeply, or whether they talk deeply because they are happy. Either way, we started thinking about how important "real conversation" is in **relationships**.

One of the perks of being in a committed relationship is the ability to discuss subjects you likely avoided during the early stages of dating or courting. So pour yourselves a drink, cozy up on the sofa and have yourselves a good heart-to-heart chat.

Marriage Tip #82

What to talk about when you are with your spouse...
Embarrassing moments – What was the most embarrassing moment of your life, this week, this month, this year?
If you can't share the awkward moments that occurred throughout high school with your partner, then who can you tell them to? Don't be afraid to broach the subject, if you haven't already. We wouldn't be surprised if our spouses stories are more horrifying (and hilarious) than yours.

Marriage Tip #83

What to talk about when you are with your spouse...
Political viewpoints - How do you really feel about the next election or that new law that passed? You don't have to agree with each other, although it would certainly help. A good relationship allows both parties to discuss their own philosophies without taking the opposing viewpoints personally.

Marriage Tip #84

What to talk about when you are with your spouse...
Fears and insecurities - By fears, we don't mean your phobia of earthworms. We're talking about things that make you wake up with gray hairs. What worries you? What do you want to improve in yourself? What are your past skeletons? In being vulnerable, you risk judgment, but more importantly, you chance finally being understood. Asking good follow up questions based on what your spouse says to you will keep the conversation going!

Marriage Tip #85

What to talk about when you are with your spouse...
Your childhoods - Ask your partner what he or she was like as a kid. Did they make friends easily? What kind of games did he or she like to play? Did they have trouble in school? Childhood memories make for fun conversations, but they can also lend insight into how your man or woman became the person they are today.

Marriage Tip #86

What to talk about when you are with your spouse...
Family ties - Knowing a person's upbringing and relationship with his or her parents (or siblings) is paramount to understanding their current attitude toward family. If you're even slightly contemplating a future with this person, it helps to ask how well they get along with their family. Why do they resent their mother or father? Why are they closer to their sisters than to their brothers? How well can they handle family gatherings?

Marriage Tip #87

What to talk about when you are with your spouse...
Current events - In the age of information overload, it's nearly impossible to stay up-to-date on everything going on around us. Here's where teamwork comes into play: Ask your partner about their interests, be they economics or regional politics, and see if you

can't learn a thing or two about them. Who knows, maybe you'll help them develop an interest in international affairs or science news.

Marriage Tip #88

What to talk about when you are with your spouse...
TV and movies - Compared to politics and personal fears, entertainment might seem pretty shallow, but classified discussions about movies in the "deep" category, given that people focused on character motivations and plots rather than on, say, the hot Hollywood leading actors.

Marriage Tip #89

What to talk about when you are with your spouse...
The future - Need we ask what's scarier or more inspiring than the future? We're not saying you should pressure your partner into talking about their plans for the marriage and children, but we do believe that whether we openly talks about them or you ask directly, you should know their dreams, goals, and aspirations. What are they working toward? What are we working toward? What drives them to succeed? Where do they see themselves in five years? Ten years? Twenty years? Planning is a prerequisite for anyone who desires to get good results. The reason many marriages are failing today is because there is no real plan of action that both spouses are aware of but have agreed upon. Someone who desires growth and is not afraid of the unknown is surely dynamic enough to deserve you. **Eleanor Roosevelt** once said, **"Great minds talk about ideas; small minds talk about people."** So, up your relationship happiness by talking about the deep stuff with your significant other.

Marriage Tip #90

Most things are not what they appear to be in marriage - The story is told of a man who left his house every night, telling his wife he was going hunting. He returned home every night about the same time, several hours after his wife had fallen asleep. Some weeks after this routine began, the wife went out to the barn one evening after her husband had supposedly gone hunting-and found his gun still there.

For several days the wife's mind ran wild; she could hardly bear to imagine what her husband might be doing during those evening hours. For almost a week she studied every word he said, every movement, every facial expression. He seems so devoted, she thought. How could he possibly be doing this to me?

Without a word, she planned her revenge. As he returned home late one evening and walked ever so carefully into the bedroom so not to awaken his wife, she stood behind the door, his gun in her hands. When her husband turned to sit down on the bed, she lifted the gun, took aim, and pulled the trigger. He never knew what hit him.

The next morning one of the first people to see the wife was a neighbor and foreman of a lumber mill several miles away. When the wife told him why she had shot her husband, the man's face froze in disbelief. **"Your husband",** he spoke slowly and deliberately, **"was working every night at the lumber mill so he could surprise you by buying you a better house."**

Not all real-life situations turn out as dramatic as this fictionalized one, of course but suspicion and mistrust in many relationships are equally as destructive.

Is suspicion and mistrust destroying your relationship / marriage right now?

Marriage Tip #91

Married couples often ask one another for favors.
Can you do me a favor?
Will you do me a favor?
Honey, do me a favor.
I want you to do me a favor.

What Are Marriage Favors? - A marriage favor is when you respond out of kindness and out of love to your spouse's request to do a something. A favor can be something as simple as fastening a necklace or picking up clothes from the dry cleaners. **If you do the favor with a "have to" attitude or begrudgingly, then you really haven't done a favor for your spouse.**

Windows of Opportunity - Try to look upon marriage favors as windows of opportunity to show your love for one another. There may be times when your spouse asks you to do the same favor over and over. This can be an "aha moment" when you recognize that this particular task is either important to your spouse or a potential problem in your marriage or both. Pay attention to these windows of opportunity. Don't throw them away.

Marriage Tip #92

Recipe For A Happy Marriage

1 cup consideration	1 reasonable budget
1 cup courtesy	3 teaspoon pure extract of "I'm sorry"
2 cupfuls flattery carefully concealed	1 cup contentment
1 gallon faith and trust in each other	1 cup confidence and encouragement
2 cupfuls praise	1 large or several small hobbies
1 small pinch of in-laws	1 cup blindness to the other's faults

Flavor with frequent portions of recreation and a dash of happy memories. Stir well and remove any specks of jealousy, temper or criticism. Sweeten well with generous portions of love and keep warm with a steady flame of devotion. Never serve with cold shoulder.

Marriage Tip #93

Although there are many ways to improve your marriage, this list of five things you can do to improve your marriage is centered around major red flag issues that can tear your marriage apart:

Lack of respect for one another

Lack of time with each other

Lack of sexual desire for one another

Lack of sharing responsibilities

Lack of having agreed upon financial goals.

10 Things Guys Wish Women Knew about Men
1) Men would rather feel unloved than inadequate and disrespected. Husbands need to know that their wives respect them both privately and publicly. Men thrive when they know that their wives trust them, admire them and believe in them. Research indicates that men would rather sense the loss of loving feelings from their wives than to be disrespected by them.

2) A man's anger is often a response to feeling disrespected by his wife. When a husband becomes angry with his wife, he may not come out and say, "You're disrespecting me!" But, there is a good likelihood that he is feeling stung by something his wife has done which he considers disrespectful and humiliating.

3) Men are insecure. Men are afraid that they aren't cutting it in life — not just at work, but at home, in their role as a husband. They may never vocalize this, but inwardly, they are secretly vulnerable. The antidote? Affirmation. To men, affirmation from their wives is everything! If they don't receive this affirmation from their wives, they'll seek it elsewhere. When they receive regular and genuine affirmation from their wives (not flattery, by the way), they become much more secure and confident in all areas of their lives.

4) Men feel the burden of being the provider for their family. Intellectually, it doesn't matter how much or little a man makes, or whether or not his wife makes more or less money in her career. Men simply bear the emotional burden of providing for their family. It's not a burden they've chosen to bear. Men are simply wired with this burden. As such, it is never far from their minds and can result in the feeling of being trapped. While wives cannot release their husbands from this burden, they can relieve it through a healthy dose of appreciation, encouragement and support.

5) Men want more sex. Everyone's natural response to this is probably, "Duh!" But, that response is probably for the wrong reason. We primarily assume that men want more sex with their wives due to their physical wiring (their "needs"). But, surprisingly, research showed that *the reason men want more sex is because of their strong need to be desired by their wives.* Men simply need to be wanted. Regular, fulfilling sex is critical to a man's sense of feeling loved and desired.

6) Sex means more than sex. When men feel their wives desire them sexually, it has a profound effect on the rest of their lives. It gives them an increasing sense of confidence and well-being that carries over into every other area of his life. The flipside of this coin also carries a profoundly negative affect. *When a husband feels rejected sexually, he not only feels his wife is rejecting him physically, but that she is somehow rejecting his life as a husband, provider and man.* This is why making sex a priority in marriage is so incredibly important!

7) Men struggle with visual temptation. This means the vast majority of men respond to visual images when it comes to women. And, this doesn't just mean the guys with wandering eyes. Even the most godly husband cannot avoid noticing a woman who dresses in a way that draws attention to her body. Even if it is just a glance, these visual images are stored away in the male brain as a sort of "visual rolodex" that will reappear without any warning. Men can choose whether to dwell on these images and memories or dismiss them.

8) Men enjoy romance, but doubt their skills to be romantic. True, many men appear to be unromantic clods, but it doesn't mean that they want to be that way! Men want to be romantic, but they just doubt their ability to pull it off. They are plagued by internal hesitations, perceiving the risk of humiliation and failure as too high. Wives can do a great deal to increase their husbands' confidence in their romantic skills through encouragement and redefining what romance looks like.

9) Men care about their wife's appearance. This isn't saying that all men want their wives to look like the latest supermodel. What men really want is to know that their wives are making an effort to take care of themselves (and not letting themselves go) because it matters to them (the husbands!). *Husbands appreciate the efforts their wives make to maintain their attractiveness.*

10) Men want their wives to know how much they love them. This was the number one response of men. Men aren't confident in their ability to express this, but they love their wives dearly. Men want to show how much they love their wives and long for them to understand this fact.

Marriage Tip #95

Don't tell your significant other that they're wrong about insignificant things. For instance, if your woman says that Steven Spielberg directed **Star Wars**, laugh a little on the inside, but don't tease her for not knowing it was George Lucas. And for the **love** of God, do not correct each other's grammar in public.

Marriage Tip #96

Speaking of being wrong, let it go when someone admits fault, especially if it's for something minor. Being able to forgive and to let go of past hurts is a critical tool for a marriage relationship. Additionally, being able to forgive is a way to keep yourself healthy both emotionally and physically.

Health Aspects of Forgiving - If you hold on to old hurts, disappointments, petty annoyances, betrayals, insensitivity, and anger, you are wasting both your time and your energy. Nursing a perceived hurt can eventually make it in to something more - hate and extreme bitterness. Lack of forgiveness can wear you down. Additionally, being unforgiving is not good for either your physical and mental well being.

How to Forgive

- Be open.
- Make a decision to forgive your spouse.
- When images of the betrayal or hurt flash in your mind, think of a calming place or do something to distract yourself from dwelling on those thoughts.

- Don't throw an error or mistake back in your spouse's face at a later date. Don't use it as ammunition in an argument.

- Don't seek revenge or retribution. It will only extend the pain.

- Accept that you may never know the reason for the transgression.

- Remember that forgiveness doesn't mean you condone the hurtful behavior.

FORGIVENESS
is not something
we do for OTHER PEOPLE.
We do it for OURSELVES
-to GET WELL and
MOVE ON.

Marriage Tip #97

Think before you speak. Whenever a difficult conversation keeps you from phrasing your thoughts coherently, ask your partner to give you a moment instead of trying to fill up the silence in the air, with whatever it is you have to say. Saying the wrong thing is much worse than an awkward break in the conversation.

Marriage Tip #98

Resentment in marriage can be tricky because it often masquerades as other emotions -- such as boredom and anger -- and has the ability to erode the quality of a marriage over time if it's not dealt with effectively. Resentment and anger often go hand in hand and are equally toxic emotions that may make people feel in control -- yet they are actually giving up control to others.

Resentment is a sneaky emotion that takes more forms that you realize. On the surface it may cause you to feel bored, or to find flaws with your partner -- picking on them for small things such as being somewhat messy or failing to return your text in a timely fashion.

Eight ways to prevent resentment from destroying your marriage:

1. **Acknowledge your feelings and practice being vulnerable in small steps** so you can build confidence in being more open with your partner. Discussing minor issues (schedules, meals) is a great place to start before tackling bigger matters such as disciplining children or finances.

2. **Be honest and communicate about key issues in your relationship.** Be sure to be forthcoming about finances, your past and concerns with a family member, co-workers, children, etc.

3. **Take responsibility for your part in the conflict or dispute**. One person's ability to do this can change the dynamic of the relationship. One spouse's response will literally change the brain waves of the other person.

4. **Apologize to your partner when appropriate.** This will validate their feelings and promote forgiveness and allow you both to move on.

5. Practice forgiveness. Forgiveness isn't the same as condoning the hurt done to you but it will allow you to move on. Try to remember you are on the same team.

6. **Show empathy to your partner.** Expressing empathy will go a long way to smooth things over -- especially after a disagreement. After he or she has shared their perception of the problem, saying something like: "I get it. It makes sense that you'd feel that way."

7. **Express thoughts, feelings and wishes in a respectful way.** Resentment can build when couples sweep things under the rug, so be vulnerable and don't bury negative feelings.

8. **Make a commitment to practice endurance and patience.** In time, many of the kinks inherent in married life will smooth out.

Marriage Tip #99

Couples who really love each other, work on understanding their partners. Some couples keep speaking the same unspoken language. We've all seen that couple at the Chinese restaurant who doesn't talk to each other? It's because they've lost their couple's language. Every happy couple has a language and we are fairly certain that long before they discovered Kung Pao chicken, they had one too. A couple's language is when you know the things your partner would find hurtful and never say them. It's also when you hear the unspoken as clearly as the spoken -- like when your partner says **"No, it's fine, really"** but you know what she's really saying is **"This is making me unhappy."**

Marriage Tip #100

Couples who love each other still surprise one another. Surprise is the best spice in the relationship casserole. Whether it's getting flowers at the office for no reason or being told to show up at the airport with just your toothbrush, surprises tell your partner you were thinking about them, missing them, and that he or she is important to you.

Marriage Tip #101

Couples who love each other understand that it's OK to do nothing for an entire weekend as long as their partner is with them. There are times when figuring out what to watch on Netflix and ordering a pizza is even too labor intensive for your current level of energy. Happy couples can just be. They can be in separate rooms, on separate floors, even one inside and one outside; it doesn't matter. They sense the other's presence and nothing becomes something. They are not bored. They are not lonely because their mate is "there."

Marriage Tip #102

Couples who love each other still recognize their partners with all five senses. Of course they see them and can pick out their voice in a crowded room. But they also know their scent, their touch and the taste of their kisses. All should be familiar; all should make your heart do a little happy flutter. Your partner's voice should do something for you.

Marriage Tip #103

Couples who love each other don't play hurtful games with their partner. They don't belittle one another for sport. They don't go out with friends for the sole purpose of bad-mouthing their mate. They've learned that hurting their partner actually devastates them. They know that their partner has the power to make them happy and conversely, make them deeply unhappy. Their partners know this too, and never abuse it.

Marriage Tip #104

Couples who love each other understand that no one needs to be always right. They don't care who's right because they and their partner are both on the same side and a win is a victory for the team. Team You Two.

Marriage Tip #105

Couples who love each other never let their partner's "stuff" annoy them to the point of rage. Dirty socks on the floor are just that. They are not an act of insult that says **"I think of you as the maid."** They aren't even **"My mother did this for my dad, so why does it bother you so much?"** No, it's more like **"Oh. Are those my socks? Yes, you're right they are. Gee, how did they get there?"** Bottom line: Don't sweat the small stuff.

Marriage Tip #106

Couples who love each other understand how to compromise without being compromised. A long happy relationship doesn't require one person to submit to the wishes of the other and then call it a day. That's the path to resentment, not a long life together. Everyone can have their own things and things they come together over.

Marriage Tip #107

It's always about the truth. Face the truth. Tell the truth. Accept the truth. Remember Rod Stewart singing about looking to find a reason to believe? If you have to look for it, it's not there. Truth is the foundation for love. And start by being true to yourself.

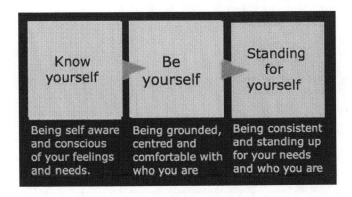

Marriage Tip #108

Highly sensitive spouses may not know that they are highly sensitive. One of the biggest sources of frustration for highly sensitive people is that they are often times not even aware that they are highly sensitive — which can cause issues to arise, particularly in marriage. But there are clues that spouses can look for to help discern if his or her partner is highly sensitive, using the acronym DOES — Depth of Processing, Over stimulated, Empathy and Emotional Responsiveness, and Subtle Stimuli. A highly sensitive person thinks deeply ... they think about the meaning of life more, they are the ones in the family who make sure they get their health check-ups. If you have children, they are the ones who run out of the room first. With husbands — they are often in their offices, for mothers, they look like they going crazy.

Marriage Tip #109

Highly sensitive spouses need alone time.
Highly sensitive people, like introverts (although the two are not interchangeable), often have a deep need for alone time, to allow their brain ample time to process, a situation that can cause frustration among married partners. When a highly sensitive spouse feels the need for downtime they should just, **"I'm taking some downtime, this is how long I will be gone."** We have to make it clear that you are not wanting time away from your spouse — but just time away from, well, everyone. Explore ways to get down time together through quiet activities, such as hiking or sitting together reading.

My life

I'm so tired of thinking. I just want to sleep.

Marriage Tip #110

Men are just as likely to be highly sensitive as women. As many men as women are born sensitive, but the stereotype is that women are sensitive, 'real' men are not."

Marriage Tip #111

Highly sensitive people view sex differently. They are more likely to find sex to be mysterious and powerful, to be turned on by subtle rather than explicit sexual cues, to be easily distracted or physically hurt during sex, and to find it difficult to go right back to normal life afterwards. Keeping an open communication going in — and out — of the bedroom can help explore some of those different needs.

Marriage Tip #112

Bedtime might be a particular crisis. You can use bedtime to illustrate the differences between a highly sensitive and non-highly sensitive spouse. A wife gets into bed only to find her brain is too overly-stimulated to sleep, while her husband is quietly snoring within minutes. Some spouses love unwinding with TV before bed, while other spouses find it way too stimulating. They just can't shut down their own brains without a nice, dark room and no screens in their presence.

Marriage Tip #113

Highly sensitive people tend to make good decisions. If you have a highly sensitive spouse, you may want to defer to them for decision-making, because although highly-sensitive people can take longer to make decisions, "they're usually good ones." She may, for instance, recall some unpleasant details about a restaurant they are considering eating at, or avoid a certain hiking trail based on past experiences, saving both parties the bane of bad bread or a less-than-dazzling view.

Marriage Tip #114

Fighting warrants special consideration for highly sensitive people. It's not a stretch to imagine that if one or both partners are highly sensitive in a marriage, fights could have the potential for disaster. For sensitive people, when you get to the point where you're really over aroused, stop and take a 20-minute break. Or better yet, try not to get to that point. We also suggest staying on the topic of what you are discussing. Don't start bringing up the other things you're mad at your partner for. If we're discussing how our children should be educated, we don't want to bring up the subject of how their mother didn't do things right. If we start throwing in the kitchen sink, then everything escalates. Being highly sensitive also might mean being more vulnerable to slights by your partner — the person who knows you best in the world. The whole goal for humans is not to be shamed — your partner knows you so well that it's easy for them to bring up the things that are shameful.

Marriage Tip #115

Recognizing that you're highly sensitive won't magically fix your marriage. Although it may feel like a bit of an eye-opener, a spouse recognizing that he or she is highly sensitive won't magically transform a relationship overnight. Couples need to get it that it's genetics, you can't change this about your partner — but you can change how you manage it. If you don't get that, you become a hard person to live with. So what's a newly informed Highly Sensitive Spouse supposed to do with all of this enlightenment? Don't go running to your spouse with the good news and don't expect your partner to be delighted with this news. You may choose to keep some of the great revelations that you find out about yourself private.

Marriage Tip #116

Make a vow from the start that you'll always be on the same team. When a conflict arises, try to remind each other that you have each other's backs and that, ultimately, we're working towards the same goal – then we can work toward finding a solution together instead of being in opposition. When we make a vow to be teammates, no matter what, we will find the strength to swallow our pride and move on from uncomfortable situations and fights so much more often. We will remember that we are not fighting because you are angry, but because you disagree, and remembering that will help keep emotions out of arguments. When you know you are on the same team, it is easier to work together to find a goal. Choosing to be teammates and making that vow aloud will do wonders for keeping your marriage intact through the tough times.

> "In every disagreement in your marriage, remember that there is not a winner and a loser. You are partners in everything, so you will either win together or lose together. Always work together to find a solution."

Marriage Tip #117

Some husbands have stopped holding their wives hand, walking by her side, opening doors for her and surprising her and taking her to nice places - Holding hands is something that married couples should be forced to do by law. I'm not kidding. After most husbands and wives are married a while, for some reason we stop holding her hand. Even after she brings this to our attention many times, something inside of us failed to act. Couples who hold hands with their spouses show the world that they love each other. They also provide strength, comfort, and affection to each other. It's very much a sign of or a silent way of saying I love you. Taking a woman's hand affords her the feeling that you honestly care about her and that you are proud to be there with her. Period. **Another thing we do as husbands is stop walking by her side.** Some husbands walk so fast that we end up half a city block ahead of our wives. Whatever we do as husbands, don't walk ahead of your lady, or drift back behind her; it's a tiny, silent 'EFF YOU!' to the person you're strolling with especially if that person is your wife. **Sometimes we stop opening doors for our wives.** It might be a generational thing, but have you ever seen in old movies how the husband always opens the door for his wife? It hurts wives when we break our necks for other women to open doors for them but we make a half-hearted effort for our own wives. This is a lost art. It is a profound act of respect. It's not that she can't open the door for herself, but it's the fact that we are putting them ahead of ourselves. We're thinking of them first. Today it's so common to run from one place to the next. Our faces are stuck to our smartphones. We seldom take these few moments to show respect to another individual - especially the most important person in our lives. We should hold doors because it's the right thing to do. There's a real genuine satisfaction and sense of pride that comes with being kind and chivalrous to a woman who we really love. Next time you are out with your wife, open her car door and go ahead and open any doors that she will walk through. You'll show her in a real simple way that she's very important to you. **Sometimes we as husbands don't take her away.** It is perfectly ok for husbands to plan romantic getaways and vacations for their wives. Some husbands have never planned a surprise weekend getaway to a local hotel and much less to somewhere like Paris. This is something that really bothers her. Put yourself in a woman's shoes. Women want to believe you're thinking about them even when you're not shoving another slice of pizza down your jaw next to her on the couch. They want be swept off their feet every once in a while by the fact that you planned a trip, just the two of you, to a place (any place really) where a married couple can walk around/drink some ice tea / hold hands / open doors for each other and maybe kiss up against the elevator door like strangers in the night. So go on, what are you waiting for?

Marriage Tip #118

Let your spouse have his/her own hobbies that do not include you. Even though you love each other, everyone needs a little break to be themselves for a bit. We are loving our spouses when we give them a break from us!

When a woman is loved correctly, she becomes ten times the woman she was before. -Reyna Biddy

Men too, deserve
to be spoiled.
Told they are handsome,
Told their efforts
are appreciated and
should also be
made to feel secure.

If he treats you like
a Queen, treat
him like a
King.

Brain your isms

Always Have
A Unique Character
Like SALT,
It's Presence
Is Not Felt
But
It's Absense Makes
All The Things
"TASTELESS"

 Marl ES
#WORDSOFWISDOM

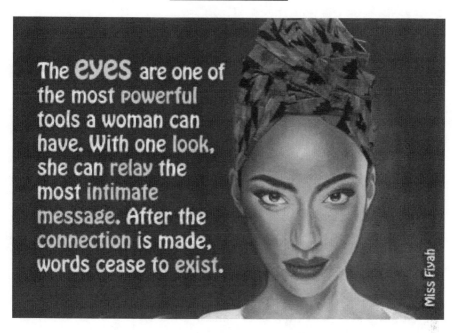

The eyes are one of the most powerful tools a woman can have. With one look, she can relay the most intimate message. After the connection is made, words cease to exist.

Miss Fiyah

But at this juncture, we would like to offer this for men who are clueless of the fascinating way in which wives communicate:

How to translate what your wife is really saying:

The wife says: You want
The wife means: You want

The wife says: We need
The wife means: I want

The wife says: It's your decision
The wife means: The correct decision should be obvious

The wife says: Do what you want
The wife means: You'll pay for this later

The wife says: We need to talk
The wife means: I need to complain

The wife says: Sure... go ahead
The wife means: I don't want you to

The wife says: I'm not upset
The wife means: Of course I'm upset you moron

The wife says: You're ... so manly
The wife means: You need a shave and sweat a lot

The wife says: Be romantic, turn out the lights
The wife means: I have flabby thighs.

The wife says: This kitchen is so inconvenient
The wife means: I want a new house.

The wife says: I want new curtains.
The wife means: Also carpeting, furniture, and wallpaper!

The wife says: I need wedding shoes.
The wife means: The other forty pairs are the wrong shade of white.

The wife says: Hang the picture there
The wife means: No, I mean hang it there!

The wife says: I heard a noise
The wife means: I noticed you were almost asleep.

The wife says: Do you love me?
The wife means: I'm going to ask for something expensive.

The wife says: How much do you love me?
The wife means: I did something today you're not going to like.

The wife says: I'll be ready in a minute.
The wife means: Kick off your shoes and take an hour nap.

The wife says: Am I fat?
The wife means: Tell me I'm beautiful.

The wife says: You have to learn to communicate.
The wife means: Just agree with me.

The wife says: Are you listening to me?
The wife means: [Too late, your doomed.]

The wife says: Yes
The wife means: No

The wife says: No
The wife means: No

The wife says: Maybe
The wife means: No

The wife says: I'm sorry
The wife means: You'll be sorry

The wife says: Do you like this recipe?
The wife means: You better get used to it

The wife says: All we're going to buy is a soap dish
The wife means: I'm coming back with enough to fill this place.

The wife says: Was that the baby?
The wife means: Get out of bed and walk him

The wife says: I'm not yelling!
The wife means: Yes I am! I think this is important!

In answer to the question "What's wrong?"

The wife says: The same old thing.
The wife means: Nothing.

The wife says: Nothing.
The wife means: Everything.

The wife says: Nothing, really.
The wife means: It's just that you're an idiot.

The wife says: I don't want to talk about it.
The wife means: I'm still building up steam.

The truth about MARRIAGE...

Most people get married believing a myth that marriage is beautiful box full of all the things they have longed for; Companionship, intimacy, friendship etc ... The truth is, that marriage at the start is an empty box, you must put something in before you can take anything out. There is no love in marriage, love is in people, and people put love in marriage. There is no romance in marriage, you have to infuse it into your marriage. A couple must learn the art, and form the habit of giving, loving, serving, praising, of keeping the box full. If you take out more than you put in, the box will be empty.

Marriage Tip #123

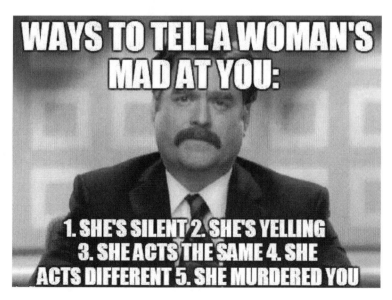

WAYS TO TELL A WOMAN'S MAD AT YOU:
1. SHE'S SILENT 2. SHE'S YELLING 3. SHE ACTS THE SAME 4. SHE ACTS DIFFERENT 5. SHE MURDERED YOU

Marriage Box

Most people get married believing a myth that marriage is a beautiful box full of all the things they have longed for: companionship, intimacy, friendship, etc. The truth is that marriage at the start is an empty box. You must put something in before you can take anything out. There is no love in marriage. Love is in people. And people put love in marriage. There is no romance in marriage. You have to infuse it into your marriage. A couple must learn the art and form the habit of giving, loving, serving, praising keeping the box full. If you take out more than you put in, the box will be empty.

Marriage Tip #125

Never stop courting. Never stop dating. Never ever take that woman or that man, for granted. When you asked her to marry you, you promised to be that man that would own her heart and to fiercely protect it. This is the most important and sacred treasure you will ever be entrusted with. She chose you. Never forget that, and never get lazy in your love. A wise man once told me that the things you do to get a woman are the things you do to keep her.... What did we use to do before we knew **"we had"** our woman? You would do anything to spend time with your mate before you said, **"I do"**...stay up all night, get up at the crack of dawn, whatever it took to have more time together. Finding time to be together was a challenge, but a welcome one. Sometimes thinking that we've got a woman on lock is the problem. Let us remember brothers that our wives are the Women of God and not the Woman of Man! A Hint to the wise is sufficient!

Marriage Tip #126

Protect your own heart. Just as you committed to being the protector of her heart, you must guard your own with the same vigilance. Love yourself fully, love the world openly, but there is a special place in your heart where no one must enter except for your wife. Keep that space always ready to receive her and invite her in, and refuse to let anyone or anything else enter there. The wise men and woman have said that when your heart is filled up with your spouse, another person cannot get in there...

Marriage Tip #127

> Be VERY careful about having friends of the opposite sex. If you have a "friend" that you tell things to that you don't tell your spouse, then you are creating toxic situation. Affairs don't start in the bedroom; they start with conversations, emails, texts and communication that lead down a dangerous path. Protect your Marriage!

Marriage Tip #128

Always see the best in your spouse - Focus only on what you love with your spouse. What you focus on will expand. If you focus on what bugs you, all you will see is reasons to be bugged. If you focus on what you love, you can't help but be consumed by love. Focus to the point where you can no longer see anything but love, and you know without a doubt that you are the luckiest man and woman on earth to be with your spouse.

Marriage Tip #129

It's not your job to change or fix your spouse... your job is to love them as they are with no expectation of them ever changing. And if they change, love what they become, whether it's what you wanted or not. Many times spouses change and forget to tell each other.

Marriage Tip #130

Take full accountability for your own emotions - It's not your spouse's job to make you happy, and they can't make you sad. Mutual accountability is essential to a healthy, harmonious union. The principles of mutual accountability require complete openness between a husband and wife. Among other things, this means: true transparency, authentic honesty, and genuine answerability. When couples are mutually accountable they allow for total access into one another's lives. They view one another as partners to be trusted and relied upon. If your goal is to have a satisfying marriage with longevity, make sure you are accountable for the part you play in the relationship — good or bad. When you are in denial about your part in the relationship then you are no better than a child flinging sand at another child in a sandbox. When you take responsibility for your part in the marriage, only then will you be able to connect with your partner in a mature, intimate way. Secrets are primary tools in dividing couples. Accountability between husband and wife is a superb way to keep them from messing with your marriage. We are responsible for finding our own happiness, and through that your joy will spill over into your relationship and your love.

Marriage Tip #131

Never blame your spouse if you get frustrated or angry with them - It is only because it is triggering something inside of YOU. They are OUR emotions, and our responsibility. When you feel those feelings take time to get present and to look within and understand what it is inside of YOU that is asking to be healed. You were attracted to this person because he / she was the person best suited to trigger all of your childhood wounds in the most painful way so that you could heal them... when you heal yourself, you will no longer be triggered by them, and you will wonder why you ever were.

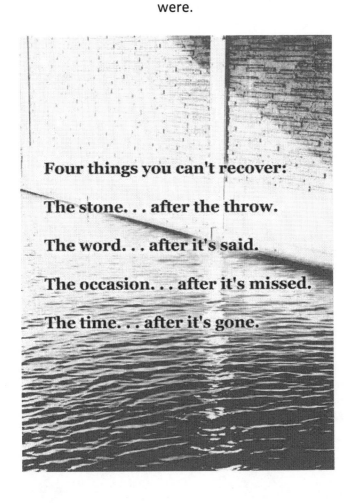

Four things you can't recover:

The stone. . . after the throw.

The word. . . after it's said.

The occasion. . . after it's missed.

The time. . . after it's gone.

Marriage Tip #132

Allow your woman to just be - When she's sad or upset, it's not your job to fix it, it's your job to HOLD HER and let her know it's ok. Let her know that you hear her, and that she's important and that you are that pillar on which she can always lean. The feminine spirit is about change and emotion and like a storm her emotions will roll in and out, and as you remain strong and unjudging she will trust you and open her soul to you... **Don't run away when she's upset.** Stand present and strong and let her know you aren't going anywhere. Listen to what she is really saying behind the words and emotion.

Marriage Tip #133

Be silly - Don't take yourself so damn seriously. Laugh. And make your spouse laugh. Laughter makes everything else easier. Laugh together. Go on adventures. Play games. Share new experiences and have fun together to boost your marriage. One of the greatest secrets to any long lasting marriage is to be honest and open and laugh whenever we can and spend time with each other.

Marriage Tip #134

Fill your spouse's soul everyday – Once you learn your spouse's love languages and the specific ways that they feel important and validated and cherished, ask them to create a list of 10 THINGS that make her feel loved and memorize those things and make it a priority every day to make them feel like a King or a Queen.

HOW TO SPEAK YOUR SPOUSE'S
LOVE LANGUAGE

WHICH LOVE LANGUAGE?	HOW TO COMMUNICATE	ACTIONS TO TAKE	THINGS TO AVOID
WORDS OF AFFIRMATION	Encourage, affirm, appreciate, empathize. Listen actively.	Send an unexpected note, text, or card. Encourage genuinely and often.	Non-constructive criticism, not recognizing or appreciating effort.
PHYSICAL TOUCH	Non-verbal – use body language and touch to emphasize love.	Hug, kiss, hold hands, show physical affection regularly. Make intimacy a thoughtful priority.	Physical neglect, long stints without intimacy, receiving affection coldly.
RECEIVING GIFTS	Thoughtfulness, make your spouse a priority, speak purposefully.	Give thoughtful gifts and gestures. Small things matter in a big way. Express gratitude when receiving a gift.	Forgetting special occasions, unenthusiastic gift receiving.
QUALITY TIME	Uninterrupted and focused conversations. One-on-one time is critical.	Create special moments together, take walks and do small things with your spouse. Weekend getaways are huge.	Distractions when spending time together. Long stints without one-on-one time.
ACTS OF SERVICE	Use action phrases like "I'll help...". They want to know you're with them, partnered with them.	Do chores together or make them breakfast in bed. Go out of your way to help alleviate their daily workload.	Making the requests of others a higher priority, lacking follow-through on tasks big and small.

Be present - Give your spouse not only your time, but your focus, your attention and your soul. Do whatever it takes to clear your head so that when you are with them you are fully with them. Treat your spouse as you would your most valuable client. They are.

"If your spouse is angry, you should be calm. When one is fire, the other should be water."

Marriage Tip #136

Be willing to take your spouse sexually - Carry your spouse away in the power of your masculine and feminine presence, to consume them and devour them with your strength, and to penetrate them to the deepest levels of your soul. Let them melt into your masculine hardness and your feminine softness as your spouse knows that they can trust you fully. When you're having sex, are you thinking about something, somewhere, or someone else? There's nothing wrong with fantasy when your spouse is in on it. But closing your eyes can sometimes send the wrong message: You're only present physically. Keeping your eyes open and looking directly into your spouses' eyes reassures them that it's them, and only them, who's turning you on in that moment. Eye contact during sex reinforces the love-making aspect of sex. It also enhances the emotional intensity and sense of intimacy.

The "revolution" starts with "love".....

BLACK WIVES MATTER!

Marriage Tip #137

Don't be an idiot - And don't be afraid of being one either. You will make mistakes and so will she. Try not to make too big of mistakes, and learn from the ones you do make. You're not supposed to be perfect, just try to not be too stupid.

The best apology is changed behavior.

Marriage Tip #138

Give her space - The woman is so good at giving and giving, and sometimes she will need to be reminded to take time to nurture herself. Sometimes she will need to fly from your branches to go and find what feeds her soul, and if you give her that space she will come back with new songs to sing. Tell her to take time for herself, ESPECIALLY after you have children. She needs that space to renew and get re-centered, and to find herself after she gets lost in serving you, the children and the world.

A million men can tell a woman she is beautiful, but the only time she'll listen is when it's said by the man she loves.

kushandwizdom.tumblr.com

Marriage Tip #139

Today, marriages and relationships in general require more skill in negotiation between partners than ever before, because there is less that is automatically accepted and more that needs to be decided. All parties involved have to increase our intelligence to make better and wiser decisions... Its a hell of a thing to continue making bad decisions year in and year out that not only complicates our lives but the lives of everyone around us including our children.

Marriage Tip #140

Be fully transparent. If you want to have trust you must be willing to share everything... Especially those things you don't want to share. It takes courage to fully love, to fully open your heart and let her in when you don't know if she will like what she finds... Part of that courage is allowing her to love you completely, your darkness as well as your light. DROP THE MASK... If you feel like you need to wear a mask around her, and show up perfect all the time, you will never experience the full dimension of what love can be.

Marriage Tip #141

Never stop growing together - The stagnant pond breeds malaria, the flowing stream is always fresh and cool. Atrophy is the natural process when you stop working a muscle, just as it is if you stop working on your relationship. Find common goals, dreams and visions to work towards.

Marriage Tip #142

DON'T WORRY ABOUT MONEY. Money is a game, find ways to work together as a team to win it. It never helps when teammates fight. Figure out ways to leverage both persons strength to win.

"A real man doesn't put his woman first. A real man puts God first because he knows that he has to follow God in order to lead his lady."

www.GodlyWoman.net

Please SHARE and Be a Blessing!

Marriage Tip #143

Forgive immediately and focus on the future rather than carrying weight from the past. Don't let your history hold you hostage. Holding onto past mistakes that either you makes, is like a heavy anchor to your marriage and will hold you back. Forgiveness is freedom. Cut the anchor loose and always choose love. "Don't return to an old grievance. Once the matter has been thrashed out let it be forgotten, or at least never allude to it again."

This is some advice that can be applied to any aspect of life. Once you've moved beyond something, *move beyond it*. Revisiting past grievances or arguments or fears will only ruin future happiness. Leave the past in the past after it has been dealt with and move forward in security.

A Happy Marriage is the union of Two Good Forgivers
-Ruth Bell Graham

Marriage Tip #144

Always choose love. Always choose love. Always choose love -
In the end, this is the only advice you need. If this is the guiding
principle through which all your choices is governed, there is
nothing that will threaten the happiness of your marriage. Love will
always endure.
In the end Marriage isn't about happily ever after. It's about effort
and a commitment to grow together and a willingness to
continually invest in creating something that can endure eternity.
Through that work, the happiness will come.
Marriage is life, and it will bring ups and downs. Embracing all of the
cycles and learning to learn from and love each experience will
bring the strength and perspective to keep building, one brick at a
time.

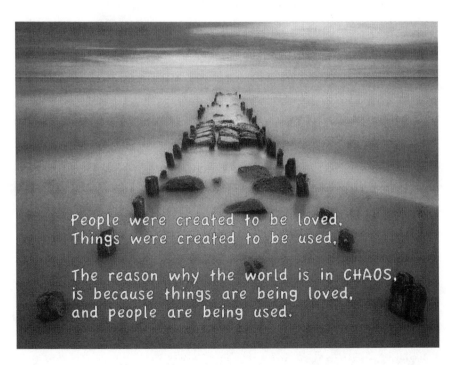

People were created to be loved.
Things were created to be used.

The reason why the world is in CHAOS,
is because things are being loved,
and people are being used.

Marriage Tip #145

Recognizing the Signs of Hidden Issues

You can't handle hidden issues unless you can identify them. There are four key ways to tell when there may be hidden issues affecting your relationship.

Wheel Spinning

When an argument starts with you thinking, "Here we go again," you should suspect hidden issues. You never really get anywhere on the problem because you often aren't talking about what really matters - the hidden issue. We have all had these arguments in which we have said everything many times before and now feel hopeless as the cycle starts yet again.

Trivial Triggers

When trivial issues are blown up out of all proportion, you should suspect hidden issues. Constant arguments between two spouses is a great example. Needing to refill an empty orange juice container seems like a trivial event, but it triggers horrendous arguments driven by the issues of power and caring.

Avoidance

When one or both of you are avoiding certain topics or levels of intimacy, or feel walls going up between you, you should suspect hidden issues. For example, we have talked with many couples from different cultural or religious backgrounds who strongly avoid talking about these differences. We think that this behavior usually reflects concerns about acceptance; Will you accept me fully if we really talk about our different backgrounds? Avoiding such topics not only allows hidden issues to remain hidden but puts the relationship at greater risk, as the couple never deals with important differences that can have great impact on a marriage. So many men have histories that set us up for emotional conflict with our wives because we have no idea of what intimacy is or looks like when displayed between a man and woman. Our father's example haunts us to this day - especially the way he handled our mothers. Some men can't remember ever seeing their parents demonstrate intimate feelings. Some of us as men have grown up with parents that never exchanged kisses, hugs, or terms of endearment and we are the same ways with our wives and children today. Some of us grew up assuming our parents loved each other because their fathers gave orders and their mothers carried them out. In our houses was where we learned the hard way to follow orders without question, too. Some of us are way too heavy handed with our children. Some of us as men always do what we are told and never express how we feel or what we want because no one ever asks us anyway. Many of us had fathers that were stoic and never showed any emotion; Maybe our fathers regarded such displays as weakness and demanded that his son(s) behave as he did. Are any of these situations in your current relationship?

Scorekeeping

When one or both of you start keeping score, you should suspect hidden issues. Scorekeeping could mean you are not feeling recognized for what you put into the relationship. It could mean you are feeling controlled and are keeping track of the times your partner has taken advantage of you. Whatever the issue, scorekeeping can be a sign that there are important things the two of you aren't talking about just documenting. Scorekeeping reflects that you are working against each other at times, rather than being teammates.

Other common but sometimes taboo topics in marriage can include issues of sex, personal appearance, feelings about ex-spouses, jealousy, and so on. There are many such sensitive topics that people avoid dealing with in their relationships out of fear of rejection. What issues do you avoid talking about?

Marriage Tip #146

Marriage is not 50-50; divorce is 50-50. Marriage has to be 100-100. It isn't dividing everything in half, but giving everything you've got!" When it comes to talking out conflicts, there is a sex difference. Some women take the attitude **"The marriage is working as long as we can talk about it."** Many husbands, on the other hand, have the view **"The relationship is not working as long as we keep talking about it..."** Can this be ever be corrected?

Marriage Tip #147

One wife discovered that what she'd been calling **"her husband's problems"** were *not* his problems after all. They were hers. The *real* problems were (1) her reactivity and (2) her reluctance to take personal responsibility. So, she practiced reframing "her husband's problem" as

- "Her problem with her own anxiety when she's a passenger and feels out of control."

- "Her problem with interpreting a reasonable request for order as a personal attack."

- "Her problem with expecting someone else to take care of her socializing needs for me."

As she started recognizing her personal preferences and expectations — **and taking responsibility for her reactions and needs — "her husband's problems" vanished one-by-one!**

With her vision no longer obscured by irritation, she began to notice her husband's countless strength's and saw all the positive contributions he was making to her life.

She finally felt free to enjoy her man and to be fully present in her marriage. She was able to give her husband **the gift of a happy wife**.

Marriage Tip #148

First of all, let's recognize that electronics – phones, tablets, computers etc, etc are just tools. We can use them for good or for bad. **Texting** is one of our favourite ways to stay connected to my hubby throughout the day when we are both busy and working. Texting is a way of saying, **"I am thinking about you. I love you. Let's stay connected."** We strive to text or to call each other several times a day just to check on each other. We are both busy and don't want texting to be intrusive, just a loving reminder that we are in this together.

Marriage Tip #149

It has been said that one mule by itself can pull two tons but that 2 mules can pull 8 tons. A husband and wife pulling together can accomplish more by cooperating with each other. Why do so many of us get caught up in power struggles?

Marriage Tip #150

Don't Triangulate - It's frightening to admit, but a couple in conflict instinctively behaves like two nations preparing for war. In each case, the warring parties create alliances in order to strengthen their respective hands. Where they differ is that a couple in a conflictual relationship sometimes develops those alliances unconsciously. In a relationship, the partner that feels the most discomfort eventually withdraws from the other and finds a third person who functions as a supportive ally.

In the lingo of marital psychology this is called triangulation. For example, a wife who is feeling lonely and cut off from her husband might increase her involvement with one or more of the children as a way of decreasing her unhappiness. A child who is especially sensitive to the suffering of one of the parents might decide to become that parent's **"caregiver."** A kid in that role almost always feels torn apart and on some level resentful about having to parent the parent.

Sometimes an acting-out teenager will unconsciously stabilize the relationship between the parents. It is as if the kid has a super radar that picks up on his or her parents' marital distress and responds by drawing each of them away from their conflict toward his drug abuse or her pregnancy or his suspension or her school failure. There is no end to the creative ways children can act out in order to divert their parents from dealing with the uncomfortable truth about their marriage.

The third person in this triangle is not always one of the children. It can be a parent, a sibling, a friend or a lover. The function of this person is to reduce the strain between the couple. For example, a man who believes that his wife has lost interest in him could conceivably reduce the tension he feels by having an affair. Until his wife finds out, the level of conflict between them will most likely subside. He also might shift his loyalty to his mother who then becomes his confidant and advisor often to the detriment of the marriage. As long as there are triangles, it's impossible for a couple to deal directly with whatever is the source of their problem. It is an obstacle to intimacy and real marital love. However, it's hard both for the partner and the third person to withdraw from their involvement with one another. In the situation of the affair, the lover might not want to end the relationship and the man may be unwilling to give up the easy intimacy of the new relationship for the difficult challenge of making his marriage work.

If the third person is a child, he or she might begin to act out as a way of re-engaging the parent. It often takes professional help from a qualified marital or family therapist to help a couple to disengage from a triangle so that it's not destructive for one or more of the people who are involved.

The cure for triangulation is trust and intimacy. The question is how does a couple whose relationship is marked by conflict, rejection and mistrust turn it around? If there's no trust, how do you develop a trusting relationship? We are going to propose the following steps to help you move in that direction:

1. One of you has to be honest about the marriage. In other words, be straight with yourself about what's missing. Write down what you would like to change in your relationship. For example, if you hardly spend any time with one another, you might write, **"I would like to spend one evening a week alone with you."**

2. Write a letter to your partner and tell him or her what's bothering you about the relationship. Avoid blaming and write about how you would like to improve the marriage.

3. In a few days, approach your partner and try to talk about what you've written. If the response is positive, then begin the work on improving your relationship. You may need professional help to succeed

Marriage Tip #151

Don't impose on your spouse's good nature. Because he / she is 'such a dear,' and will give you anything you like to ask for, don't take advantage and ask for something unreasonable. Kindness is a virtue that can be spoiled by exploitation. When you are making requests of your significant other, be sure that you are being reasonable. Good things are ruined if you take advantage of them so just because your spouse says they don't mind doing you a favor doesn't mean you should ask them for that favor over and over again. Eventually, they might mind and it might mean bad news for your marriage.

Marriage Tip #152

Best Relationship: Talk like best friends, play like children, argue like husband and wife, protect each other like brother and sister.

Marriage Tip #153

A happy marriage is a balancing act of meeting your own needs and each other's needs. Listen, be present in the moment, and think before you speak, but don't lose your sense of self in the process of giving. Keeping a hold on who you are and what you want to do with your personal life when you are married to another individual is a vital step in finding and maintaining happiness in a marriage. You must balance out your own needs with your spouse's needs. You must find a way to connect and relate and be there for one another while sharing your separate lives together, without meshing them into one life. Finding that balance when you are giving and taking is crucial to finding success in your marriage.

Marriage Tip #154

"Are you still mad at me?"
"No."
"Are you sure?"
"I was never mad at you."
"What were you?"
"Hurt."

Marriage Tip #155

It takes too much energy to spend your whole life covering up feelings to prove that you are independent, assertive, controlled, courageous, competitive, and carefree at all times. It takes much less energy to reveal who you really are and, in turn, have someone love you for your vulnerabilities as well as your strengths...Brothers let's stop shutting our women out of our lives...

Marriage Tip #156

This one is difficult for most spouses: **"Don't take your partners negativity to seriously"**... Successful couples attack problems, not each other. The unsuccessful couple is entrenched in negativity and don't want to give each other a single break...

Marriage Tip #157

Brothers listen to your Wife's advice. God has given you a **"second opinion"** in your Wife, so listen to her and take heed. As you have already seen in your marriage, **"Two heads with two minds are much, much better than one"** You'll be glad you did! This is also vice versa! Wives listen to your Husband's advice too! Especially when he knows what he is talking about!

"Marriage is a not a noun; it's a verb.
It isn't something you get.
It's something you do.
It's the way you love your partner every day."
Barbara De Angelis
Lindaloycelones.com

Marriage Tip #158

Don't become a mere echo of your husband. If you never hold an opinion of your own about anything, life will be dreadfully colorless for both of you, and there will be nothing to talk about. Part of being married is sharing interests outside of your relationship. When you have your own life, your own priorities, and your own activities going on – you have things to talk about when you get home at night. If you become an echo of whatever your spouse is interested in, you won't ever truly be happy because you won't be living a life that is true to yourself. Avoid this pitfall by keeping up with your own hobbies and interests outside of your marriage.

Marriage Tip #159

Don't be jealous of your husband's acquaintances with other women. You don't want him to think you are the nicest woman in the world because he never sees any others, but because he sees plenty, and still feels that you are the only one in the world for him. In order to have a happy, healthy marriage, you both need to have lives outside of your marriage. You both need friends and acquaintances to lean on and to spend time with — people that you aren't married to. Don't allow jealousy into your marriage because it will be the downfall of your relationship. Remember that it is important to maintain barriers and some of those barriers include allowing your spouse to have friends outside of your relationship. After all, if you are truly in love, you should be able to trust your partner and trust that his friendships outside of your marriage are honest.

Marriage Tip #160

Give more than you take. – When you shift your attitude from **"how can I gain"** to **"how can I give,"** you'll be amazed at the gifts you receive from each other. In a way, when you give each other everything, it magically becomes an even trade; each wins all. Marriage is not a noun, it's a verb. It isn't something you get, it's something you do. It's the way you love your partner…

Marriage Tip #161

You've probably heard the expression **"self-fulfilling prophecy."** Well, it applies here. If you're negative about the prospects of your marriage, your partner and the whole world will sense it, making it more likely that your efforts won't get off the ground.
If you concentrate hard on always finding the silver lining — even if you have to fake it til you make it — your good attitude will help fuel your rekindled romance.

Marriage Tip #162

Unhappy marriages consist of unhappy people. Although marital unrest can lead to individual unhappiness, it also works the other way around… If you are dissatisfied with your own life, everything is colored by that fact. Little irritants spark major crises. We've got a shorter fuse with the children and we're more likely to respond rashly to our mates… when our own life is in order, we feel better about ourselves, which helps us to be more clear headed about our marriages…

Marriage Tip #163

Help them stay focused on the positive. Your spouse had 7 billion people in the world to choose from and they chose you as a husband or a wife. Why? What was it about them that was so special you decided to pledge 'til death do us part'? Remind them of those things. In that moment when they are frustrated and they want to focus on everything you are doing wrong, lovingly listen to them and then remind them of everything you do right. Remind them of all the things that they have shared over the years about what makes you great. Sometimes marriage is like being too close to the trees to see the forest. You can help remind your spouse of what beauty is in the forest all around them.

Marriage Tip #164

Help your spouse change their thought that marriage is "hard work". Most of us are underpaid and underappreciated for the work we do. When you call marriage "work," you subconsciously tell yourself you are giving more than you are receiving. But when you use words like "effort" or "investment," there is an expectation there will be a reward. The more effort you put in the more reward you will get out. The more investment you put it, the larger the dividend that pays out. By helping your spouse change their phrase, *"marriage is hard work,"* to *"marriage takes effort,"* you have just changed how your spouse sees their marriage.

Marriage Tip #165

Flaws and mistakes don't make the person. We all have husbands and wives who make mistakes, who are flawed and make seemingly thoughtless decisions at times. The funny thing, is we often forget that we have flaws and make mistakes too. By lovingly reminding your spouse that she is flawed, just like you are, she can gently be reminded that we're all a little crazy. And having someone willing to put up with our craziness is worth the effort.

Marriage Tip #166

When you first start courting someone, there is a mixed bag of emotions including butterflies, excitement, and a sense of mystery. As time goes on, your relationship transitions to long-term status, and the initial happiness of the "honeymoon" phase can wear off. Just because you've been with someone for what feels like forever doesn't mean the relationship has to become stale. **Challenge yourselves** and the relationship! Check out these 50 tips to help **keep the romance well and strong** for many more years to come.

Plan a **date night**.

Take a trip together.

Try a new hobby as a couple.

Go out on a double date.

Surprise your significant other.

Take some "me" time.

Communicate your feelings.

Discuss the future.

Support one another's dreams.

Don't go to bed angry.

Make a **bucket list** together.

Try something new, yet righteous in the bedroom.

Get a couple's massage.

Team up in the kitchen and cook a new recipe.

Do something to show your significant other you care.

Remind her she's beautiful or that he's handsome.

Be honest about your feelings on a hot-button topic.

Respect one another.

Sign up for a class together.

Don't hold on to past grudges.

Make time for friends and family.

Do something you've never done before together.

Take a breather when you're fighting so you don't say something you'll regret.

Joke around with each other. Laughing is good for the soul.

Put an equal amount of effort into the relationship.

Mix up your evening routine by playing a board game.
Reminisce about your first date.
Have more sex.
Talk about an issue you've been sweeping under the rug.
Take time to really listen.
Be patient with one another.
Make time for one another as a couple.
Plan a spontaneous getaway.
Write a romantic letter or note.
Make breakfast in bed.
Plan an amazing date night at home.
Do something special for your anniversary.
Say "I love you" more.
Clean the house together.
Flirt with one another.
Focus on the positives instead of the negatives in your relationship.
Unplug for a night. No TV, computers, or phones.
Don't sweat the small stuff.
Do something you're scared of together.
Show some love.
Encourage one another to take on new challenges.
Take a bubble bath together.
Dress up for a date night.
Read a book together and talk about it.
Never forget why you fell in love in the first place.

Marriage Tip #167

Whoever said, **"Sticks and stones may break my bones, but words can never hurt me"** must have never been told a rude word, or never went to high school. Words hurt, and they can leave scars with us that are difficult to heal. We are not perfect and we occasionally react in ways we wish we could take back. Every husband and wife will drop the ball and prove themselves fallible time and time again. The conviction that a marriage must be perfect makes a marriage fragile. When we expect perfection, we often get nothing. Sometimes we say things that are hurtful and that we don't truly mean. Other times, we don't even realize the things we are saying to another person can be damaging. We aren't aware of our passive aggressive tone, or that we don't need to bring up that one subject again. All of this goes for being in a relationship, as well. It's normal for couples to argue and to get into heated debates, but we do need to eliminate some words from our vocabulary. Communication is key for a relationship to be strong and healthy. With that being said, you want to communicate in an effective way, instead of using words that might stir up emotions.

Marriage Tip #168

Hurtful Names - Some people get down and dirty when they are upset. Whether it's a learned style of fighting from their childhood or they watched one too many episodes of the Sopranos — it needs to stop. Calling your partner words like, "Bitch" or "Asshole," isn't going to help any situation. It will only make you and your loved one lose respect for one another.

Marriage Tip #169

Don't use silence as a weapon - Silence is a deadly weapon. It's easier to deal with a non-violent, verbal fight where at least you get out what's bothering you than an icy silence where all you can do is imagine how many different ways your partner hates you. So, if you don't want to kill your relationship, then you need to learn how to express resentments in a way that can be heard, acknowledged and resolved. That skill is of utmost importance in a relationship; without it, small problems become major catastrophes. So, how do you learn to say all those things that are so hard to say? And, how do you say them to a partner who may tell you to go take a flying leap? Granted, it's not easy but making a relationship work never is. Try the following and get back to us and tell us what happened.

1. Write a list of your resentments in the following way: **"I resent you for x."**
2. Write a letter to your partner about what's bothering you. Don't blame. Try to start from a positive, loving place. An example might be:

"Dear Kareem, I feel a real need to talk about us. I love you and want our marriage to work. What I'm about to tell you might hurt you. It's not my intention. What I want is for us to be close. But there are things I want to get off my chest. Please think about what I'm writing and try hard not to react with anger. This is hard for me but here goes:

I am upset with....."

Don't dump the kitchen sink on your partner. Mention a few of the most important things that are bothering you. If you are aware of what your part is in creating problems, mention it. Your partner will be much more open to looking at his part if he feels you're doing the same.

Marriage Tip #170

Don't say yes when you mean no - We're often afraid to say no to our partners. Perhaps, you're scared that they'll become angry, or, maybe, if you were to say **"I'm sorry, I just don't want to do that,"** they'd be disappointed and you'd start feeling guilty. So, instead of asserting ourselves and saying what we want, we end up doing the opposite and often feel resentful. The problem with saying yes when we mean no is that we stop being real in the relationship. There's no intimacy in a relationship without honesty. It may be that when you start to say no when you mean no, you'll say yes when you mean yes. Your honesty might increase the trust in your relationship. More likely, however, the change in your behavior will at first be threatening to your partner. Remember he's not used to you being so honest. She might be painfully surprised to learn that not all of your yes's were indeed yes's. It's important to know that anytime you change the rules in a relationship there's bound to be conflict. That's okay. Conflict is often necessary for a relationship to grow. Through conflict two people can create a deeper understanding of one another and develop a stronger bond. If you already have a strong connection with your spouse, then your commitment to honesty will only deepen that relationship. If you don't, I recommend you proceed carefully. Before you start being totally honest, try to assess what your partner's reaction will be. Perhaps the most effective way of asserting yourself is to speak to your partner about how you feel and insist that the two of you get professional help. The process of reaching a deeper level of honesty is often bumpy, but once you arrive, it's well worth it.

Write the following on a piece of paper: **"I'm afraid to tell my partner...."** Prioritize the list, one being the easiest of your truths to reveal, two, the second easiest and so on. Imagine approaching your partner and telling him or her, the truth. Notice how you feel as you do that. Try breathing easily and gently tell yourself to relax. When you're able to visualize speaking to your partner, then take the risk of doing it in reality. Start with the easiest (1) and go down your list.

Saying yes just to please someone else isn't a true yes. It's not good for them, and it's not good for you.

Marriage Tip #171

"You Can't Do This Or That" - The word "can't" should only be spoken by your angry parents, not by your romantic partner. In a relationship, there will be times where you wish your significant other didn't do certain things, like go out with his or her friends on date night or spend the rest of the grocery money on shoes. You will want to tell them they "can't do that." The problem is, we are not in charge of our partner. So by using the word "can't" only makes us sounds controlling. Instead, express how it feels when your other half does a, b or c.

Marriage Tip #172

Don't play shrink. In other words, **"Don't interpret!"** Don't assume you understand your partner's deepest motivations and the subtlest nuances of his behavior. You may think you're objective, but nobody who is deeply involved in a relationship can maintain professional distance. More often than not, interpretations don't come from a place of selfless concern and a desire to help. Rather, if we're honest with ourselves, we'd recognize that these so-called truthful statements about our spouse are just disguised resentments, cloaked in a garment of objective concern.

Many spouses don't want their partners to interpret what they think and feel. They want them to listen and to hear. They would like their spouse to respond as a friend, as someone who is concerned about them. There are two antidotes to interpretations: The first is to be clear about our resentments and not to express them covertly through our analysis of our partner's behavior. The second is to listen in an open, loving manner.

The next time your partner talks to you, work extra hard at trying to understand her. Practice active listening by non-verbally indicating that you're hearing him. You can do this by maintaining eye contact and holding your partner's hand or embracing him / her in a caring, non-sexual manner. Periodically, respond with supportive statements that acknowledge how your partner feels. An example might be, **"I understand how angry you are at your boss. If I were you, I'd sure be furious."**

Marriage Tip #173

Don't mind-read - Don't assume that you know what your partner is thinking and feeling. There's a good chance you could be wrong, and wrong assumptions cause unnecessary conflict.
Imagine this situation. You walk into the living room and there's your husband sitting on his favourite chair glaring at the wall. His lips are tight; his jaw is clenched. Your immediate reaction: fear.
"What did I do? Why is he so angry at me?" You tentatively approach him, **"What's the matter, Abdul?"** you ask, expecting him to pour his wrath upon you. Abdul slowly turns toward you. The tense, angry look begins to melt and he says sadly, **"I've been laid off."** **"Well...Thank God,"** you almost blurt out, **"at least it wasn't me."** In this case, the woman checked out her assumptions and found out that her husband wasn't upset with her. Yet how often does it happen that we make the wrong assumptions and just go on believing them without ever discovering if they're true? It often happens during the process of marital therapy that assumptions, illusions and fantasies are exposed as false or only partially true. For example, the angry, critical husband who supposedly hates his wife might in fact be an insecure man who is convinced that his wife doesn't love him. Perhaps, as in one case that I know of, a distant, rejecting wife turned out to be a very sad woman, mourning the loss of her mother. So, to quote a basic training drill sergeant, ***"Assumptions are the mother of all f-ups."*** Don't assume. Check it out. Take a piece of paper and without thinking too much about it, complete the following sentence: **"I assume that my partner thinks or feels.... about me."** After you compile your list, try checking out some of these assumptions.

Marriage Tip #174

"You're just like my ex." It can be all too tempting to compare your current object of affection to people you've dated or courted in the past. But bringing up ex-loves has a time and a place. It's rarely a good idea to tell your current flame that his / her negative qualities **remind you of your ex**. On the other hand, there's absolutely room in a close relationship to talk about how you were hurt in the past. In fact, love is defined by **openness and honesty** about our thoughts and feelings. If your current long-term partner is legitimately doing something that reminds you of a painful past experience, try explaining how you were wronged and suggesting how your significant other could tweak his or her behavior.

Marriage Tip #175

Don't take your partner for granted - Think about this question for a moment. Are you as polite, kind and considerate to your partner as you are to a casual acquaintance? For most of us, the answer is no. How come? How is it that this same person that we now hardly give a moment's thought to, unless it's negative, could be the same one to whom you once were so loving, giving and appreciative? Let's face it. We're all guilty of amnesia. After a time, we just seem to forget about all those small and large kindnesses that our partners do for us. Or, if we don't forget, we just come to expect that it's part of our partner's job description. When a relationship reaches the point at which amnesia or expectation replaces appreciation, then trouble is close at hand.

But, we can change that with our spouses! We can start by not assuming that those things that our partner does for us are obligatory. In fact, we would suggest you take a piece of paper and write down those things that your partner does for you - both large and small. Then honestly ask yourself, among those things that your partner does for you, do you ever show appreciation and in what manner do you express it? Most likely, you'll discover that for many of the kindnesses on the list you've probably never said **"Thank you. I really appreciate you for..."** So if you would like to breathe some life into your relationship, let us suggest the following. Try committing yourself to a week of thank you's and notice the change.

Marriage Tip #176

"You always (or you never)..." These general statements are almost never productive in a conversation. Instead, they just serve to put your significant other **on the defensive**. Using words such as "always" or "never" when you're trying to get your point across to your significant other, will do just quite the opposite — get your point nowhere. Sometimes it gets frustrating that your partner doesn't do exactly what we were hoping they would. Whether it's cleaning up after they eat, or spending more quality time with you — it's how you communicate that will get your message through. When you start out a sentence with "you never," never expect them to be receptive. You've already put them straight into defense mode because it sounds like an attack. These all or nothing words exaggerate what is actually occurring and even worse, send your partner into defense mode. So if you tell him he never introduces you to his friends, he'll come back with that time he brought you to meet his entire family. Strive to zero in on a specific issue (you didn't introduce me to any of your friends at the party tonight), and how it made you feel (I felt embarrassed), and what he or she can do differently next time (introduce me to at least one person, and I'll take it from there). Instead, put it in a positive spin by saying "I would appreciate if you would do a, b or c. Maybe it was just an oversight for your spouse. Maybe you just have to learn not to take everything that happens in the relationship so personal.

Marriage Tip #177

"You can't afford that!"- If you are maintaining separate finances, it's probably best to stay out of your partner's affairs. For one thing, telling him or her what he or she **can and can't afford this or that** might make your partner see you as an authority figure — and nothing screams "sexy" like an image of Mom or Dad. And many people consider their finances a crucial part of their ego and identity. But if you are managing your money together and you feel he or she is spending it unfairly, consider expressing your concern in a calm, sensitive way. Starting from a **"we"** standpoint, instead of "you." So try: **"Can we talk about *our* financial plans**?"

1. Examine your current financial situation

2. Develop your financial goals

3. Complete an analysis

4. Provide recommendations

5. Implement your financial action plan

6. Review & update your financial plan periodically

Financial Planning **Process**

Marriage Tip #178

"The sex was great" (if it wasn't) - Maybe you're fibbing because you don't want to hurt your partner's feelings about his or her sexual prowess. But, getting **truly intimate** with someone means admitting that not everything between you two is perfect. Try being honest and telling your partner that no, you didn't orgasm this time, but you have some ideas about how to bring out the fireworks next time you two get together. There's a good chance he or she will be more than willing to try them.

Marriage Tip #179

Marriage and media - Movies offer a wealth of affirmation inspiration! The next time you watch a flick with your spouse, look for specific ways he or she excels in tasks and traits illustrated in the movie. For example, is there an absent father figure in the show? Wives, whisper in your husband's ear how wonderful of a dad he is. Is there a pretty actress on cast? Husbands, make your wife blush by verbally praising her beauty. Compliment each other during the movie, and watch your spouse glow long after the credits stop rolling!

Marriage Tip #180

"**Relax!**" Even if someone isn't your significant other, he or she probably never wants to hear these words. When you're stressed, the last thing you want to feel is that someone close to you thinks you're overreacting or **acting crazy**. Telling your other half to "relax" if he or she is upset, is like asking them to get 10 times more upset. When you say comments like, **"You're making a big deal out of nothing,"** it only invalidates your partner's feelings. People feel how they feel. So instead of lessening how he or she feels, try to understand where he or she is coming from.

Instead of trying to force your partner to act or feel differently, try some sympathy: **"I'm just as upset about this as you are. Let's deal with it together."** If you have children, take them on a field trip to give your spouse a moment of solitude. Example trips for an afternoon include ice cream parlors, park playgrounds, museums – many which have free or discount admission days – and zoos. It can work as a great bonding time for you with your children, while also allowing your spouse to relax, unwind and not have to worry about taking care of anyone.

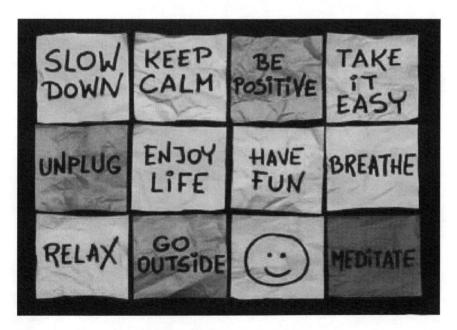

Marriage Tip #181

"Your parents are terrible." Because anyone who's seen Monster-in-Law knows this situation is totally a possibility. In reality, **surveys suggest that 75 percent of couples fight with their in-laws, so** there's a good chance that you and your significant other's mom aren't exactly besties. We get it, you don't love the fact that his mother always has to give her two cents about your relationship. No matter how much your partner's family members annoy you, keep your feelings to yourself. Family is family and they are here to stay. Be careful what you say about them because they are never going away. You know what they say, **"Keep your friends close, but your partner's family members closer."** The solution to this problem isn't to keep things hidden from your partner. Instead, you should make your partner aware of how his or family is treating you. Focus on how you feel (hurt, betrayed, frustrated), instead of all the mistakes the family made. And remember, be respectful. Think about how you'd want your partner to talk about your family if the situation were reversed.

Marriage Tip #182

"Stop asking if you're fat." There are probably a million sarcastic ways to answer the question, *"Honey, does this garment make me look fat?"* But **body-image issues** are serious, and if you really care about your partner, you shouldn't take those issues lightly. Instead of dismissing his or her comments and questions, try responding in ways that show your significant other you like him or her just as he or she is. (**"I don't think you look fat in those jeans. You look sexy as usual to me."**)

If the comments continue, consider being blunt and telling your partner that he or she needs to learn to accept him or herself. A statement like, **"You are worth so much more than your looks to me and to others"** can be pretty powerful, if you mean it.

Marriage Tip #183

Every marriage has its bumps, and they can pop up at any time. What's important is that you learn to navigate them smoothly—before they send your relationship into a ditch.

No matter how far along the marriage highway you've gone, there are some simple, fundamental rules of the road. Putting them into practice isn't always easy, but it's critical. If you do play by the rules, you'll make your marriage stronger, and the good stuff—fun, sex, trust, affection—will be better than ever.

1. Build up your love balance - Boredom, frustration and everyday irritations can douse the spark between you and your spouse—and more of the same certainly won't feed the flame. Making the good stuff your top priority will. Here's how to do it:

First, consider that it takes up to 20 positive statements to outweigh the harm done by one negative one—or by a steely squint or impatient "humph." So do more of the former, less of the latter. Compliment your wife on her new shoes, or your husband on his new blue shirt. Thank him for helping around the house. Dial her office for a quick "thinking of you" check-in (don't discuss household chores or bad report cards).

Be sure these compliments and thank you's are heartfelt and specific: **"I can always count on you to make sure my car is safe and ready to use." "This new tablecloth is nice—you're always thinking of ways to make our home pleasant."** Make eye contact when you smile or deliver a compliment. Try a little joyful noise (a happy sigh, say) when giving a loving touch.

Once you take this approach, you'll realize that, in addition to knowing how to push Mr. or Mrs. Right's hot buttons, you know how to push his or her joy buttons too (and we don't just mean sex). After all, that's how this whole thing started. It won't be long before you appreciate that it's always the right time for small acts of love. Give him a *"glad to see you"* hug and kiss when you get home. Surprise her with coffee in bed on a rainy Sunday (then stay to talk). Revel in the best qualities; let faults slide. Flash your **"I'm so happy we're here together"** smile as you trek the recycling bin to the curb. Resolve to enjoy a long kiss before you turn in each night. You do little things for your children. Why not for your spouse? Marriage is about knowing your spouse's buttons and choosing not to push them. **Let the wife make her husband glad to come home, and let the husband make his wife sorry to see him leave.**

Marriage Tip #184

Reach out - Human touch aids the release of feel-good endorphins, for giver and receiver. So link arms as you walk into the grocery store. Brush her cheek with your fingertips when you smooch good morning. Revive the ways you touched in the early days—a kiss on the back of the ear, a hand through her hair. Touch is a complex language. It pays to improve your vocabulary.

Adding more of this kind of touch will help you build a fortress of love. That's important, because a couple who form a tight unit can weather any storm (and are better able to stave off infidelity). How do you build this bond? First, support your soul mate. Take his or her side whenever possible if trouble arises in the "outside world." Keep your spouse's secrets to yourself, even when everyone at work spills theirs. Except in a true emergency, don't let anything interrupt "us" time. That's what voice mail and bedroom-door locks are for.

Speaking of "us" time: Make a commitment to spend up to 30 minutes a day chatting with each other about everyday plans, goals and, yes, dreams. One rule: no household-management or "what about our relationship" talk. This is time to build a friendship. Studies show that being friends pay off over time, ensuring a closer, sexier union. And don't forget to make time for intimacy, even if you must log it in your day planner. Schedule sex? Absolutely, if necessary. Spontaneity is great, but if either of you hungers for affection or physical love, don't wait for that special moment.

Another thing you shouldn't wait for: chances to celebrate success. Super Bowl victors. World Series champs. Gold-medal skiers. They all have one thing in common: When they win, they party. And even small victories deserve recognition. If your marriage is humming along, that alone is worth celebrating. Dine out where you proposed. Or book a midwinter-deal trip to another, warmer state or country. You've earned it.

Marriage Tip #185

Remember—nobody's perfect - It's tempting to blame your spouse when you feel angry, disappointed, bored, betrayed or stressed out about your marriage. Then it's a short hop to seeing your mate as the one who must change for the marriage to improve. That's a cop-out. Trying to improve your spouse puts him or her on the defensive and casts you in a dreary role. The result? Nobody changes. Nobody takes responsibility. Everyone is unhappy. And making your spouse the bad guy means ignoring the 90 percent of him or her that's good. The true fix: Change yourself. When you address your own flaws and seek the best in your spouse, magic happens. Optimism increases. Your spouse feels better because he or she feels appreciated, not chastised. And you both feel motivated to change in ways that lead to even more joy.

One tip to help get you thinking this way: Adopt the Japanese philosophy of imperfection, wabi sabi ("wah-bee sah-bee"), which applies well to real-life love. Next time your guy or gal does something annoying, take a breath, mutter "wabi sabi" and remind yourself that his or her intentions are good, even if the execution isn't. At the same time, don't ignore what's good in your spouse. Each day this month, pick something, big or small, that you like about him or her. Then name it. For example: **"My wife is thoughtful"** or **"My husband makes me laugh."** Then think of a specific act that backs it up: **"She made sure dinner was the bomb last week." "If I'm feeling down, he'll joke me out of it."**

Finally, honor your own imperfections. Sometimes we blame ourselves for all that's off kilter in our marriage. Too much guilt can paralyze. So, think of qualities you value, tell yourself you have them and think up real-world examples. **"I am loving and kind—I gave my spouse the last cookie yesterday." "I am honest—I tell her what I'm really thinking."**

Marriage Tip #186

Add some zing - The classic advice experts give to singles seeking a perfect match: Be **"the one"** to attract **"the one."** Same goes in marriage. The happier you feel, the happier your marriage will be, and the easier it will be to manage conflicts. If 15 minutes of morning yoga, a switch to decaf, or a new hobby gives you a relaxed zing, the good feelings can't help but lead to happier, richer moments together.

Maybe it's time to spruce up your look. Try a new look by doing something different with your hair, brush your teeth and throw on a new robe. Feeling good about the way you look makes your eyes sparkle. You're more likely to make eye contact. That sends a spark to your spouse. You know what to do next!

A bad attitude is like a flat tire. You can't go anywhere until you change it.

Marriage Tip #187

Always fight fair - Conflict is a normal, even healthy, part of any marriage. What's important is how you handle it. In a Florida study of longtime couples, joint problem-solving ability was cited as a key factor for 70 percent of satisfied pairs; just 33 percent of unsatisfied couples had mastered this skill. With the right tools and attitude, conflict becomes a gateway to deeper intimacy—the chance to be seen and loved for who you truly are, to accept your mate's adorable, vulnerable real self, and to build a strong union without caving in or silently seething.

First, steer clear of criticism, confrontation and hostility. They're like gas on a fire. University of California researchers who followed 79 couples for more than a decade found that early divorcers fought long and loud and were always on the attack—or the defensive.

Happy couples, on the other hand, avoid verbalizing critical thoughts, keep discussions from escalating, and don't use absolutes like **"never"** and **"always."** If a fight does start, try to change the subject, inject gentle humor, empathize or show your spouse extra appreciation. **Express your appreciation.** – Sometimes people don't notice and appreciate the things others do for them until they stop doing them. Don't do this to yourself or your partner. Too late? Call a truce, walk away and cool off for a while.

Marriage Tip #188

Pick the right time and place - Don't start potentially tough talks if you're not well rested and well fed. Hunger and fatigue can unleash nasty remarks and dark thoughts. Don't ever try to deal with serious marital issues if you've got one eye on something else. Turn off the TV, the phone, the laptop. Close the catalog. If you're distracted or going out the door, pick another time to talk. You can't resolve conflicts on the fly.

Remember, too, that how you handle these situations doesn't just affect you. Is the conversation G-rated? Will it end happily? If not, stop and reschedule for when the children aren't around. When they are, keep things respectful and productive. Research shows that children thrive (and absorb good relationship skills) when parents resolve issues constructively, but develop insecurities and behavior problems when exposed to hopeless shoutfests.

Marriage Tip #189

Open your ears - The single most powerful step you can take to keep a marriage solid? **Speak less and listen more.** Blame, insults, criticism and bullying predict a bad end, or at least a living hell. When talk turns combative, don't interrupt, offer a solution or defend yourself too soon. When feelings are at issue, they need to be heard. So nod, rephrase or provide a soft "um-hum" to show you honor the emotions behind the words. Sometimes, all we really need to do to feel closer to someone is pay closer attention to what it is that they're saying.

Marriage Tip #190

Share the housework - Research finds that couples that split household duties, including cooking, cleaning and child rearing, enjoy more sex and are happier than couples where the woman tackles "feminine" tasks and the man tackles "manly" tasks. Married couple who enjoy the pleasures of the table have, at least once a day, a pleasant opportunity to be together. The person who cooks shouldn't do the dishes. It's only fair! If you are able, do everything as a team. Use the teamwork concept around work outside the home and also in the home, with raising the children. Teamwork should be very instrumental in your marriage. Our marriages are not going to make it if we don't have great teamwork between the two spouses. If the wife has the attitude of, **"I don't need my husband to be successful"** and the husband also feels that he doesn't need his wife to be successful then it's no wonder we are having so many problems...Too much independent thinking and actions is causing the destruction of many marriages... Isn't your spouse's success tied to your success and vice versa? Don't we still need each other to survive? Let us strive to talk with each other versus at each other about just what we are doing each and every day.... Let us stop yelling at each other when we communicate... Many of us are behaving as if we haven't been taught anything.

Marriage Tip #191

All you need is love - A majority of successful couples say love makes their marriages successful. Saying it to each other and remembering it can help strengthen relationships. Anyone who does not have a lot of disagreements in a marriage is probably repressing a lot of stuff, which is liable to explode sooner or later. Are we strong enough in love to disagree with one another? Loving each other is really just the beginning. There are three keys to marriage and they are all very difficult to forge.

The first is good communication which requires practice, goodwill, determination and a considerable amount of inborn talent.

The second is respect, which in many ways is more important than love. Love comes and goes, but respect endures, and provides the space for love to flow after the ebb, which is bound to come in all long marriages sooner or later.

The third is trust. And this is the hardest of all, because if you have ever been let down – and we all have – reconstructing the trust is difficult. This isn't about infidelity, but many small matters – broken promises, bad intentions, frustrated hopes. You have to trust, even though you have no guarantee you won't be let down, and then, if you are let down, trust again, and then again. You must keep doing this as long as you are humanly able to, and your marriage will either stand or fall on it. This requires what we call the power of "forgettory" as opposed to memory. You need to forget and forget again about any perceived hurts and mistreatment. Dragging the weight of the past behind you will drag you down in the end.

But you will never, can never, "get there", because there is nowhere to get to. A marriage is a moving process, a living thing, and if it stops being fed with these existential nutrients, it will finally expire. Complacency and laziness is what kills marriage, far more than lack of love, and that is why it is often described as hard work. But no work is ultimately more rewarding.

Marriage Tip #192

Pack your bags, but not your children - While parenting feels fulfilling, sometimes taking a break from the children and focusing on each other is greatly needed. It helps couples re-join and allows children to gain some independence. We decided to start taking vacations without our children because we knew almost immediately that it was important for us to stay connected. You probably should go away mostly for weekend trips. The location doesn't matter much. It really is about being exclusively together. Remember though men, when we as fathers are involved in the parenting process it strengthens the family unit and enriches our children, our wives and ourselves as men...

Marriage Tip #193

Have fun together - Laugh together. Go on adventures. Play games. Share new experiences and have fun together to boost your marriage. We think the secret to our marriage is to be honest and open and laugh whenever we can and spend time with each other.

Marriage Tip #194

Go to bed angry if you want to. It has often been said that a couple should never let the sun set on an argument, but this is a bit unrealistic. **A sure way to stop a red-hot argument is to lay a few cold facts on it.** Some arguments are, by their nature, two-day events: too much is at stake to set an arbitrary bedtime deadline. Faced with a stark choice between closure and a night's sleep, you're better off with the latter in almost every case. We've gone to bed angry loads of times, with no particular deleterious effects. You don't actually stay angry. It's a bit like going to bed drunk; you wake up feeling completely different, if not better.

Marriage Tip #195

Marriages and other long-term relationships have a significant public element. Like an iceberg, the bulk of a marriage is hidden from view, but the top bit, the bit that you take out to parties and show off, should appear exemplary to outsiders: charming without being cloying; happy without being giddy; entertainingly spiky, but also mutually respectful. Above all, the whole thing should look effortless. Everybody knows marriage is hard; no one wants to watch you do the work. I'm not saying that faking it in public is the key to marital success, but if you get this front-of-house stuff wrong, it will eventually have an impact on your actual relationship.

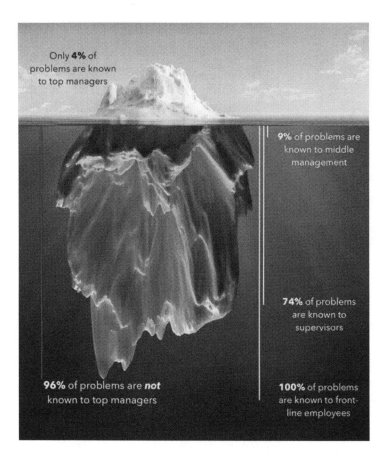

Only **4%** of problems are known to top managers

9% of problems are known to middle management

74% of problems are known to supervisors

96% of problems are **not** known to top managers

100% of problems are known to front-line employees

Marriage Tip #196

Don't make the time you spend together too special. Spending time together is important, but it shouldn't feel important, otherwise it creates undue pressure to enjoy the time. You don't have to go on a mini-break or light candles every time. Doing normal, everyday things as a couple counts as relationship maintenance, much in the same way that hovering counts as exercise. Walking together, eating dinner together and wandering aimlessly through a shopping precinct together counts. Many couples are so busy that they don't take time to nurture the foundation of their marriage and their relationship with each other. As we know all too well, when that marriage foundation begins to crumble, everything else comes down with it.

Men, you would never think of ignoring your car for a year at a time, so why do you think your wife can go for days or weeks at a time without attention from you? Women, you wouldn't think of buying a plant and refusing to water it, so why do you think your husband can go for days or weeks without some of his most important needs being met?

We all need to get away alone and continue to talk, laugh and have fun together. It's in those times of **courting** your mate that true connection takes place. We need to learn more about each other, our past and our dreams for the future. We need to feel at ease with each other as we face new challenges together. That's why courting shouldn't stop with marriage.

Marriage Tip #197

When it comes to questions such as **"How do I look in this?" "Do sideburns suit me?" "Are these trousers all right?"** and **"Do you like my new hair cut?"** everyone, male or female, appreciates something that sounds like an honest answer. This is not necessarily the same as an honest answer. We have to learn how to be honest without being offensive. **Remember that** honesty **is the basis of all** healthy relationships. Honesty gives rise to **trust**, which is essential for maintaining relationships. Honesty also establishes consistency, allowing the other person to rely on what you say as carrying true meaning. Most importantly of all, honesty is about respect and valuing the dignity of the other person.

Marriage Tip #198

Don't go out on Valentine's Day. As far as relationships go, February 14 is amateur night, and you have nothing to prove. Book a table for the 13th instead; you'll have the restaurant to yourselves.

Marriage Tip #199

Naturally there is a lot of disagreement in a partnership, but make certain you're on the same side when battling outside forces: money; unfeeling authority; intractable bureaucracy; strangers who have parked stupidly. Mindless solidarity is vital under these circumstances – fight side by side, or run away together giggling, but don't be divided. We should be adamant about this principle in our home with our spouses! Children today are very, very smart...

"Can I go to dad and get a different answer? Is what mom telling me not important because Dad is disputing her while she tells me? What should I believe?"

Are you a united front in front of your children and how do you work this all out with your spouse when, perhaps your views on different issues are not in alignment?

Talk with your partner, set up expectations and basic guidelines.
Do not undermine the others authority.
Talk in private when you do not agree with a decision.

Many marriages would be better if the husband and the wife **clearly understood** that they are on the same side.
-Zig Ziglar

Ziglar.com

Marriage Tip #200

Every partnership is unique: you should not feel the need to judge the success of yours in comparison to other relationships you see out there. For the most part, whatever you do to make it work between you is fine, even if no one else seems to handle things in quite the same way. You're even entitled to cherish your relationship's quirks and odd accommodations. These things are in the best of marriages and relationships.

During tough times it can be very tempting to compare your relationship with your spouse, with your friends, family member's or even your parents relationship to their spouse. To you, it may seem as though they have the perfect marriage or the perfect spouse. You may even think that something is wrong with your marriage or spouse, because your relationship is not as great as theirs seems. While these couples are happily floating along in their marriage, you feel like your swimming against the current. Don't compare your marriage to other couples—you never really know what goes on behind closed doors.

About your authors:

Brother Marcus and Sister Cecelia have been in the process of marriage for the last 23 years. You can access them at www.marcusandcecelia.com or call 770-256-8856.

Made in the USA
Columbia, SC
08 June 2024

36324540R00098